Lonely Planet

Pocket
BARCELONA

TOP SIGHTS • LOCAL LIFE • MADE EASY

Regis St Louis, Sally Davies

In This Book

QuickStart Guide

Your keys to understanding the city – we help you decide what to do and how to do it

Need to Know
Tips for a smooth trip

Neighbourhoods
What's where

Explore Barcelona

The best things to see and do, neighbourhood by neighbourhood

Top Sights
Make the most of your visit

Local Life
The insider's city

The Best of Barcelona

The city's highlights in handy lists to help you plan

Best Walks
See the city on foot

Barcelona's Best...
The best experiences

Survival Guide

Tips and tricks for a seamless, hassle-free city experience

Getting Around
Travel like a local

Essential Information
Including where to stay

Our selection of the city's best places to eat, drink and experience:

⊙ **Sights**

✕ **Eating**

🍷 **Drinking**

✪ **Entertainment**

🛍 **Shopping**

These symbols give you the vital information for each listing:

♪ Telephone Numbers		🚼 Family-Friendly
⊙ Opening Hours		🚌 Bus
P Parking		⛴ Ferry
⊖ Nonsmoking		Ⓜ Metro
@ Internet Access		Ⓢ Subway
📶 Wi-Fi Access		🚊 Tram
🥗 Vegetarian Selection		🚆 Train

Find each listing quickly on maps for each neighbourhood:

Bar Hemingway

16 🍷 Map p233, B2

Legend has it that Hemi self, wielding a machine ...rate this timber-pan ...ered bar during ...showpiece is a ...en by Papa ar ...town. Dress ...s.com; Hôtel Rit ⊙6.30pm-2a

6 ⊙ Plac
...V

Lonely Planet's Barcelona

Lonely Planet Pocket Guides are designed to get you straight to the heart of the city.

Inside you'll find all the must-see sights, plus tips to make your visit to each one really memorable. We've split the city into easy-to-navigate neighbourhoods and provided clear maps so you'll find your way around with ease. Our expert authors have searched out the best of the city: walks, food, nightlife and shopping, to name a few. Because you want to explore, our 'Local Life' pages will take you to some of the most exciting areas to experience the real Barcelona.

And of course you'll find all the practical tips you need for a smooth trip: itineraries for short visits, how to get around, and how much to tip the guy who serves you a drink at the end of a long day's exploration.

It's your guarantee of a really great experience.

Our Promise

You can trust our travel information because Lonely Planet authors visit the places we write about, each and every edition. We never accept freebies for positive coverage, so you can rely on us to tell it like it is.

QuickStart Guide 7

Explore Barcelona 21

The Best of Barcelona   143

Barcelona's Best Walks

Barcelona's Best ...

Survival Guide   177

QuickStart Guide

Welcome to Barcelona

One of the world's most captivating cities, Barcelona is a whirlwind of madcap Modernista architecture, sun-kissed beaches and lamplit medieval lanes hiding brilliantly creative dining and drinking dens. The storied Catalan capital has a treasure chest of historical and artistic riches, from ancient Roman ruins to Picasso-filled galleries. Soaring Gothic cathedrals, roaring FC Barcelona matches and late nights in vintage cocktail bars – are just a few of the many experiences awaiting in Barcelona.

View over Barcelona
ALLAN BAXTER/GETTY IMAGES ©

Barcelona
Top Sights

La Sagrada Família (p108)

A temple as much to originality in architecture as to God, the recently consecrated La Sagrada Família is Gaudí's Modernista masterpiece and an extraordinary work in progress.

Park Güell (p114)

The playfulness of Gaudí's imagination takes flight in this park, which seems to spring from a child's fantasy of seriously weird structures and larger-than-life animal forms.

La Catedral (p28)

Barcelona's cathedral spans the centuries like a sombre and silent witness to the city's history. It's a towering edifice of singular and monumental beauty with a refined cloister inhabited by geese.

La Rambla (p24)

Few pedestrian thoroughfares can rival La Rambla as it cuts a swathe through old Barcelona and down to the edge of the Mediterranean. It's a canvas, a catwalk and a stage all in one.

Basílica de Santa Maria del Mar (p62)

This soaring Gothic church is a study in grace, harmony, symmetry and simplicity, and is a prime candidate for the title of our favourite traditional house of worship in the city.

Casa Batlló (p92)

Gaudí outdid himself with this fantastical creation on Barcelona's grandest boulevard. With its shimmering coloured tiles and mask-like balconies, Casa Batlló evokes a dragon, a riotous festival and an undersea kingdom all in one.

Museu Picasso (p58)

Pablo Picasso's enduring gift to the city he loved is this superb collection of the artist's early works – an intriguing study of Picasso's search for a style all his own.

Mercat de la Boqueria (p46)

One of Europe's great produce markets, this is also the centrepiece of Barcelona's culinary culture. You'll find buzzing tapas bars and uniquely Catalan produce all under one roof.

Museu Nacional d'Art de Catalunya (p118)

Home to Barcelona's finest art collection, this museum has Romanesque treasure from the Catalan Pyrenees, Venetian Renaissance masters and Catalan art.

La Pedrera (p90)

Architecture becomes high art in Gaudi's final civil project. The brilliant Modernista apartment block is a showcase of extraordinary and thoughtful details, from the organic door handles to the centurion-like chimney pots.

SANTI RODRIGUEZ/SHUTTERSTOCK ©

KRZYSZTOF DYDYNSKI/GETTY IMAGES ©

Fundació Joan Miró (p122)

There is no finer or more comprehensive collection of Joan Miró's artistic endeavours than this museum. Miró is one of Barcelona's favourite sons and was a towering figure of 20th-century Catalan art.

Camp Nou & the Camp Nou Experience (p136)

In a city of temples and sacred turf, few rival the home of FC Barcelona for the passion it arouses. It's one of the greatest sporting stadiums on earth and a place of pilgrimage.

Barcelona Local Life

Insider tips to help you find the real city

If you're eager to experience Barcelona rather than merely tick off its iconic sights, we'll show you how the locals experience their city – vintage-filled tapas bars and flea markets, Catalan traditional dances and local drinking holes that haven't changed in decades.

A Barri Gòtic Sunday (p30)

▶ Local markets
▶ Traditional dance

In the most heavily visited part of the city, locals reclaim their *barrio* (neighbourhood) on Sundays. Join them at a mass in the 14th-century church where Gaudí was once arrested, then enjoy back-to-basics markets, visit icons of Catalan power and discover timeless local eating haunts.

Revelling in El Raval (p48)

▶ Bastions of tradition
▶ Gritty streets

El Raval is Barcelona's most diverse neighbourhood, at once stylish and slightly louche in the manner of port cities down through the centuries. From the refined to the bohemian, it's a journey through cultures and countercultures with detours to ageless Catalan classics en route.

Tapas & Bar-Hopping in El Born (p64)

▶ Tapas bars
▶ Nightlife

So much of life in Barcelona as the locals experience it revolves around food, and El Born, a tight tangle of medieval streets near La Ribera's southern edge, is one of the best (and prettiest) places in town to go out for tapas and drinks.

Barceloneta Sea & Seafood (p78)

▶ Fish restaurants
▶ Beaches

A bulwark of busy bars and fish restaurants where old-style cooking prevails, the former fisherfolk district of Barceloneta has held fast to its traditions. But the shiny new Barcelona has grabbed hold of the surrounding beaches and marinas. These are two very different worlds in one city.

Shopping in the Quadrat d'Or (p94)

▶ Designer boutiques
▶ Gourmet shops

One of Europe's grand shopping boulevards, Passeig de Gràcia is

Platja de la Barceloneta (p79)

stage to the city's top fashion boutiques. But L'Eixample's genius is to throw up a whole culture of shopping, with the greatest affections reserved for local names in design, furniture and high-quality foodstuffs.

Village Life in Gràcia (p112)

▶ Old-style plazas
▶ Markets & bars

Though on the cusp of downtown, Gràcia feels like a world removed from the big-city bustle. Narrow lanes, peaceful plazas and a tightly knit neighbourhood vibe lends the whole place a village-like feel. You'll find a vibrant mix of old and new, with old-

fashioned markets, bars and restaurants alongside a new wave of designer boutiques and creative tapas bars. Gràcia is diverse and offbeat – just how the locals like it.

Nightlife in Sant Antoni & Poble Sec (p124)

▶ Terrace bars
▶ Tapas

Just below the looming mountain of Montjuïc, the pedestrian lanes of Poble Sec are dotted with tapas joints and bohemian drinking dens. The action continues across wide Av del Paral·lel, in Sant Antoni, with outdoor cafes and creative tapas bars.

Other great places to experience the city like a local:

Barri Gòtic cafes (p40)

Antic Hospital de la Santa Creu (p51)

Beach bars (p86)

Parc de la Ciutadella (p68)

Speakeasy (p102)

Filmoteca de Catalunya (p55)

Passadís del Pep (p70)

Carrer de Blai (p132)

Sarrià (p139)

Aire de Barcelona (p74)

Barcelona
Day Planner

Day One

☼ Begin with Barcelona's standout sight, the otherworldly **La Sagrada Família** (p108), getting there early to avoid the queues. After a couple of hours (or more) acquiring a taste for Gaudí's flights of architectural fancy, head over to **La Pedrera** (p90) and **Casa Batlló** (p92). Have a browse in the antique-filled **Bulevard dels Antiquaris** (p106), then enjoy a tapas lunch at **Tapas 24** (p101).

☀ After lunch, stroll the length of **La Rambla** (p24), then dive into the narrow lanes of Barcelona's oldest quarter, the Barri Gòtic. Begin in **Plaça Reial** (p34), move on to the **Església de Santa Maria del Pi** (p34), then finish up at **La Catedral** (p28), but otherwise simply wander to get lost.

☾ As evening approaches, have a snack and some *cava* (sparkling wine) at **El Xampanyet** (p65), follow it up with some creative tapas at **Bar del Pla** (p65), then move on to the enduringly popular **Cal Pep** (p65). Anywhere along Passeig del Born is great for night-time revelry, but the outdoor tables at **La Vinya del Senyor** (p73) offer mesmerising cathedral views.

Day Two

☼ Get an early start at the **Mercat de la Boqueria** (p46), wandering amid the market stalls and perhaps stopping for breakfast at **Bar Pinotxo** (p47). It's always worth checking out the exhibitions at **MACBA** (p51) and the **Centre de Cultura Contemporània de Barcelona** (p51). Stop off for a hot chocolate at **Granja M Viader** (p49) and lunch at **Flax & Kale** (p52).

☀ **Palau Güell** (p51) is a wonderful way to start the afternoon. After an hour there, head across the old city to the sublime **Basílica de Santa Maria del Mar** (p62) for an hour of quiet contemplation, followed by a couple of hours at the **Museu Picasso** (p58), one of Barcelona's most rewarding museums.

☾ Candlelit **La Vinateria del Call** (p35) is a great old-city choice for a sit-down Catalan meal, followed by tea in atmospheric **Salterio** (p40). Otherwise, make an early tapas stop at **Belmonte** (p36) and head for an uplifting live performance at the **Gran Teatre del Liceu** (p27). Afterwards take a nightcap in lively **Ocaña** (p40) on Plaça Reial.

Short on time?
We've arranged Barcelona's must-sees into these day-by-day itineraries to make sure you see the very best of the city in the time you have available.

Day Three

☀ After an early-morning stroll down **La Rambla** (p24), drop off its southern end to La Rambla del Mar for a seaside stroll. Pause for a lesson in Catalan history at the **Museu d'Història de Catalunya** (p82), then dive into the old fishing district of Barceloneta, emerging on the other side for a walk along the beach. For lunch, have a seafood feast with waterfront views at **Barraca** (p86).

☼ For some of the best views in Barcelona, take the **Teleférico del Puerto** (p181) cable car across to Montjuïc. The area's museums, vantage points and gardens are all worth exploring, but a couple of hours each at the marvellous **Fundació Joan Miró** (p122) and **Museu Nacional d'Art de Catalunya** (p118) will keep you busy all afternoon.

☾ At the foot of the Montjuïc hill, **Quimet i Quimet** (p132) is one of our favourite tapas bars in town. Afterwards, have a drink at bordelloesque **El Rouge** (p125), then stroll over to **Bar Calders** (p125) in Sant Antoni.

Day Four

☀ Use the morning to immerse yourself in two of Barcelona's most iconic (if very different) sights: the weird and utterly wonderful playground-like **Park Güell** (p114), where Gaudí's fertile imagination ran riot, and a stadium tour at the home of FC Barcelona, **Camp Nou** (p136). Both are worth a couple of hours. Afterwards head up to Sarrià for a meal at **Vivanda** (p140) and a wander through the village-like lanes.

☼ Head back to the old city for a tour of the **Palau de la Música Catalana** (p68) and spend some time soaking up the neighbourhood market feel of the **Mercat de Santa Caterina** (p68). Hop on the metro up to L'Eixample's Passeig de Gràcia for some of Europe's best **shopping** (p94). Spend some much needed downtime over a velvety red wine at **Monvínic** (p95).

☾ A last night in Barcelona deserves something special: a splurge at the Michelin-starred **Cinc Sentits** (p104) or the Gaudí-decorated **Casa Calvet** (p104). After a refined cocktail or two at **Dry Martini** (p105), take one last stroll down **La Rambla** (p24) to bid farewell to the city.

Need to Know

For more information, see Survival Guide (p177)

Currency
Euro (€)

Language
Spanish, Catalan

Visas
Generally not required for stays of up to 90 days (not at all for members of EU or Schengen countries). Some nationalities need a Schengen visa.

Money
ATMs widely available. Credit cards accepted in most hotels, restaurants and shops.

Mobile Phones
Local SIM cards can be used in unlocked European and Australian phones. Other phones must be set to roaming.

Time
Western European Time (GMT/UTC plus one hour, or plus two hours during daylight savings).

Plugs & Adaptors
Plugs have two round pins; the standard electrical current is 220V.

Tipping
Small change (€1 per person in restaurants) and rounding up (in taxis) is usually sufficient.

① Before You Go

Your Daily Budget

Budget less than €60
▶ Dorm bed €17–28
▶ Set lunch from €10
▶ Bicycle hire per hour €5

Midrange €60–200
▶ Standard double room €80–140
▶ Two-course dinner with wine for two €50
▶ Walking and guided tours €15–25

Top End more than €200
▶ Double room in boutique and luxury hotels €200 and up
▶ Multicourse meal at top restaurants per person €80
▶ Concert tickets to Palau de la Música Catalana around €50

Useful Websites

Miniguide (www.miniguide.es) Restaurants and bars, upcoming events and theatre reviews.

Barcelona Metropolitan (www.barcelona-metropolitan.com) New restaurant openings, nightlife reviews and city profiles.

Barcelona Turisme (www.barcelonaturisme.com) City's official tourism website.

Lonely Planet (www.lonelyplanet.com/barcelona) Destination information, hotel bookings, traveller forum and more.

Advance Planning

Three months before Book hotel and reserve a table at a top restaurant.

One month before Check out reviews for theatre and live music and book tickets.

One week before Browse the latest nightlife listings, art exhibitions and other events to attend while in town.

② Arriving in Barcelona

Most visitors arrive at Aeroport del Prat (www.aena.es), 12km southwest of the city. Some carriers land at Aeroport de Girona–Costa Brava (www.girona-airport.net), 90km north of Barcelona. The main train station is Estació de Sants, 2.5km west of La Rambla.

✈ From Aeroport del Prat

Destination	Best Transport
Barri Gòtic	A1 Aerobús; Metro (line 3)
El Raval	A1 Aerobús; Metro (line 3)
La Ribera	A1 Aerobús; Metro (lines 1, 4)
Barceloneta	A1 Aerobús; Metro (lines 1, 4)
L'Eixample	R2 Nord Train

✈ From Aeroport de Girona–Costa Brava

Destination	Best Transport
Barri Gòtic	Barcelona Bus; Metro (lines 1, 3)
El Raval	Barcelona Bus; Metro (lines 1, 3)
La Ribera	Barcelona Bus
Barceloneta	Barcelona Bus; Metro (lines 1, 4)
L'Eixample	Barcelona Bus; Metro (lines 1, 3)

✈ At the Airports

Aeroport del Prat Terminal 1 and 2 arrivals halls have ATMs and tourist information.

Aeroport de Girona–Costa Brava The baggage-claim and arrivals halls have ATMs.

③ Getting Around

Barcelona has an efficient and comprehensive public transport system. Apart from getting into town from the airport, the metro (www.tmb.net) is the best way for getting around town. For some outlying areas, the metro is supplemented by the FGC (www.fgc.net) suburban rail network. Conveniently, both operate under the same ticketing system (as do city buses); it works out cheaper to purchase the 10-trip T-10 ticket (€10.30) rather than buying individual tickets.

Ⓜ Metro

Eight colour-coded metro lines criss-cross central Barcelona. Metro stations circle the old city (the Barri Gòtic, El Raval and La Ribera), and the metro leaves you on the perimeter of Barceloneta. There are also stations all across L'Eixample.

🚌 FGC

The suburban rail network is particularly useful for Pedralbes, Sarrià and Gràcia. Stations in the town centre include Passeig de Gràcia and Plaça de Catalunya.

🚋 Funicular

A funicular railway (part of the metro) connects Paral·lel metro station to the stations up the hill in Montjuïc; these additional stations are part of the Telefèric de Montjuïc, require separate tickets, and carry you to the summit. The Teleférico del Puerto (cable car) connects Barceloneta with Montjuïc.

🚕 Taxi

Taxis can be hailed on the street or you can call for one. Taking a cab across town can be convenient outside peak traffic times.

🚲 Bicycle

Barcelona has over 180km of bike lanes. The city has numerous bike-hire outlets, but note that the red 'Bicing' bikes are for local residents only.

Barcelona
Neighbourhoods

Park Güell ◉

Worth a Trip
◉ **Top Sights**

La Sagrada Família (p108)

Park Güell (p114)

Worth a Trip
○ **Local Life**

Village Life in Gràcia (p112)

Camp Nou, Pedralbes & Sarrià (p134)

Home to FC Barcelona, a 14th-century monastery, and Sarrià, Barcelona's loveliest village.

◉ **Top Sights**

Camp Nou & the Camp Nou Experience

La Sagrada Família

La Pedrera ◉

Casa Batlló ◉

Camp Nou & the Camp Nou Experience ◉

La Rambla ◉

Mercat de la Boqueria

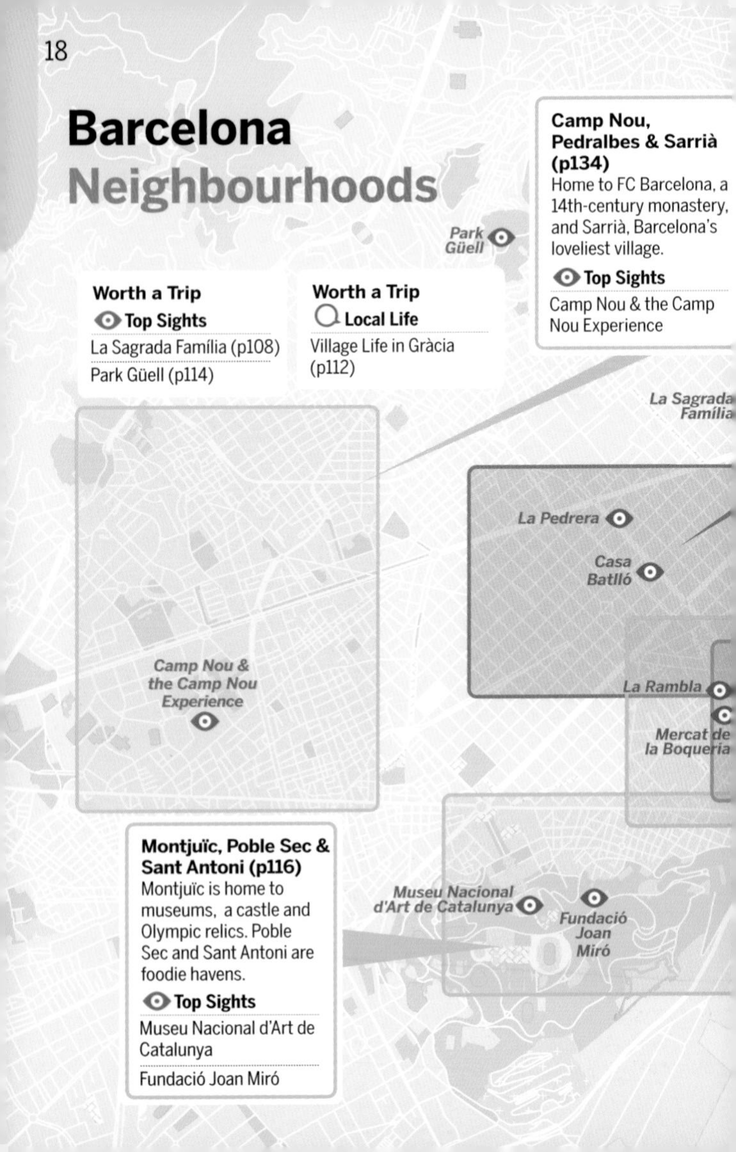

Montjuïc, Poble Sec & Sant Antoni (p116)

Montjuïc is home to museums, a castle and Olympic relics. Poble Sec and Sant Antoni are foodie havens.

◉ **Top Sights**

Museu Nacional d'Art de Catalunya

Fundació Joan Miró

Museu Nacional d'Art de Catalunya ◉

Fundació Joan Miró ◉

Passeig de Gràcia & L'Eixample (p88)
Explore Modernista treasures, outstanding bars and restaurants, and a shopper's paradise to rival Paris.

⊙ Top Sights

La Pedrera

Casa Batlló

La Ribera & Parc de la Ciutadella (p56)
La Ribera has a wonderful market, splendid architecture, plus El Born district – Barcelona's byword for cool.

⊙ Top Sights

Museu Picasso

Basílica de Santa Maria del Mar

Museu Picasso

⊙ *Basílica de Santa Maria del Mar*

⊙

Catedral

Barceloneta & the Beaches (p76)
Barcelona as it once was with an age-old culture of fishing, and an altogether shinier new beach culture.

La Rambla & Barri Gòtic (p22)
Barcelona's old quarter combines famous La Rambla with narrow medieval streets and monumental buildings.

⊙ Top Sights

La Rambla

La Catedral

El Raval (p44)
The former port district includes a fabulous market, bars and restaurants, stunning art galleries and an unlikely Gaudí confection.

⊙ Top Sights

Mercat de la Boqueria

Explore
Barcelona

Worth a Trip

Platja de la Barceloneta (p79)
VISIONS OF OUR LAND/GETTY IMAGES ©

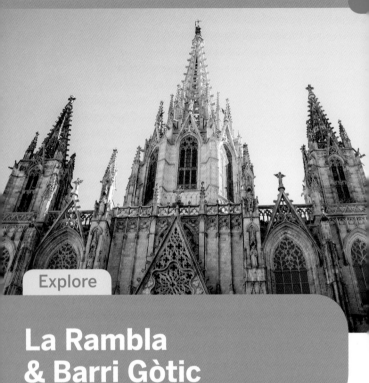

Explore

La Rambla & Barri Gòtic

One of the world's most celebrated thoroughfares, La Rambla is an essential Barcelona experience. Crouched along its eastern flank, the Barri Gòtic (Gothic Quarter), which dates back to Roman times, is packed with narrow atmospheric lanes, hidden squares and striking medieval architecture. It's a delight to explore, with historical treasures (plus charming cafes, shops and eateries) lurking around every corner.

The Sights in a Day

 Start your day as early as possible with a stroll down **La Rambla** (p24), then head for **La Catedral** (pictured left; p28); the sooner you get here after opening time the better. Depending on how long you linger, you probably have time for a morning visit to the **Museu Frederic Marès** (p34), punctuated by a coffee in its outdoor cafe.

After a lunch of traditional Catalan cooking at **Cafè de l'Acadèmia** (p36), lose yourself in the labyrinth of the old quarter. The city's Roman heritage makes a fine theme on which to focus your meanderings, stopping in at the **Museu d'Història de Barcelona** (p34) and passing by the **Temple Romà d'August** (p34). And on no account miss the **Església de Santa Maria del Pi** (p34).

As night falls, **Plaça Reial** (p34) is a fine place to begin your evening, particularly at **Ocaña** (p40). After a meal at **Belmonte** (p36) or **Pla** (p38), catch a show at **Jamboree** (p42) or **Gran Teatre del Liceu** (p27). End the night with bespoke cocktails and fine grooves at laid-back **Ginger** (p39).

For a local's day in the Barri Gòtic, see p30.

 Top Sights

La Rambla (p24)

La Catedral (p28)

 Local Life

A Barri Gòtic Sunday (p30)

 Best of Barcelona

Catalan Cooking
Cafè de l'Acadèmia (p36)

Belmonte (p36)

La Vinateria del Call (p35)

Bars
Ocaña (p40)

Sor Rita (p40)

Getting There

Ⓜ **Metro** This is the best option. Catalunya station (lines 1, 3, 6 and 7) sits at the top of La Rambla; Liceu (line 3) is at La Rambla's; while Jaume I (line 4) sits on the Barri Gòtic's eastern perimeter.

Ⓜ **Metro** Drassanes station (line 3) is at the waterfront end of La Rambla.

Top Sights
La Rambla

Everyone walks La Rambla during a Barcelona stay. In just a 1.25km strip you'll encounter food stalls, flower stands, street performers, grand public buildings, a pungent produce market, pickpockets, prostitutes and a veritable United Nations of passers-by. More than anywhere else this is where the city's passion for life as performance finds daily expression, as a relentless tide of people courses down towards the Mediterranean in a beguiling counterpoint to the static charms of Gaudí's architectural treasures.

Map p32, B5

Ⓜ Catalunya, Liceu, or Drassanes

Crowds on La Rambla

Don't Miss

La Font de Canaletes
From Plaça de Catalunya, La Rambla unfurls down the hill to the southeast. Its first manifestation, La Rambla de Canaletes, is named after the pretty 19th-century, wrought-iron fountain La Font de Canaletes. Local legend has it that anyone who drinks from its waters will return to Barcelona. More prosaically, delirious football fans gather here to celebrate whenever FC Barcelona wins.

Església de Betlem
A little further to the southeast, the early 18th-century **Església de Betlem** (☎93 318 38 23; www.mdbetlem.net; Carrer d'en Xuclà 2; ☻8.30am-1.30pm & 6-9pm; Ⓜ Liceu) was once the most splendid of Barcelona's few baroque offerings. Its exterior still makes a powerful impression, but arsonists destroyed much of the interior at the outset of the Spanish Civil War in 1936. Approaching Christmas, check out the *pessebres* (nativity scenes).

Flower Stalls
La Rambla's assault on the senses continues along La Rambla de Sant Josep (named after a now-nonexistent monastery), which extends from Carrer de la Portaferrissa to Plaça de la Boqueria. For much of its length, La Rambla de les Flors (as it is popularly known) is lined with flower stalls, assailing passers-by with heady fragrances to accompany the gathering clamour.

Palau de la Virreina
The Palau de la Virreina is a grand 18th-century rococo mansion set back ever so slightly from La Rambla's western border. It houses the **Centre de la Imatge** (☎93 316 10 00; www.ajuntament.barcelona.cat/lavirreina), an avant-garde exhibition space with rotating shows that focus on cutting-edge photography.

☑ Top Tips

▸ Keep a close eye on your belongings at all times – pickpockets love La Rambla as much as tourists do.

▸ Take an early-morning stroll and another late at night to sample La Rambla's many moods.

▸ Unless you're prepared to pay up to €10 for a beer, avoid the outdoor tables along the main thoroughfare.

▸ The balconies of the Museu de l'Eròtica have marvellous views of the Mercat de la Boqueria's entrance.

✗ Take a Break

For a proper sit-down meal, your best nearby bet is at one of the many restaurants ringing Plaça Reial (p34).

The best spot for breakfast – or coffee at any time of day – is the **Café de l'Òpera** (Map p32, B5; ☎93 317 75 85; www.cafeoperabcn.com; La Rambla 74; ☻8.30am-2.30am; 🛜; Ⓜ Liceu).

Catalunya Ⓜ
C. dels Tallers
C. de Santa Anna
La Font
de Canaletes
C. de la Canuda
ⓘ
Església
de Betlem
C. de la Portaferrissa
C. del Carme
Palau de la
Virreina
Mercat de la ◉
Boqueria
◉ Museu de l'Eròtica
Flower
Stalls
C. de l'Hospital
◉ Mosaic de Miró
Ⓜ Liceu
Cafè de
l'Òpera
La Rambla
C. de Ferran
C. de Sant Pau
Gran
Teatre
del Liceu
◉ Plaça
Reial
C. Nou de la Rambla
◉ Ocaña
C. dels Escudellers
C. de l'Arc del Teatre
Centre
d'Art Santa
Mònica
Av. de les Drassanes
Ⓜ
Drassanes
La Rambla
◉ Museu
de Cera
◎ 0 ————— 100 m
Plaça del
Portal de
la Pau
◉ Mirador
de Colom

Mercat de la Boqueria

Restaurant chefs, office workers and tourists all stroll amid the seemingly endless bounty of this hallowed market (p46). Discover glistening fruits and vegetables, gleaming fish counters, dangling smoked meats, pyramids of pungent cheeses, barrels full of olives and marinated peppers, and chocolate truffles and other sweets. Scattered about, a handful of popular tapas bars serve up delectable morsels.

Museu de l'Eròtica

Barcelona takes pride in being a pleasure centre and the **Museu de l'Eròtica** (Erotica Museum; ☎ 93 318 98 65; www.erotica-museum.com; La Rambla 96; adult/concession €9/8; ⊙ 10am-midnight; Ⓜ Liceu), a private collection devoted to sex through the ages, falls somewhere between titillation, tawdriness and art. Exhibits range from exquisite Kama Sutra illustrations to early porn movies, S&M apparatus and a 2m wooden penis.

Mosaïc de Miró

A little further along lies an oft overlooked mosaic by the great Catalan artist Joan Miró. The circular work embedded in the pavement features his characteristic simple motifs in bold colours of blue, red and yellow. Miró himself chose the location for the mosaic, which lies not far from Passatge del Crèdit, where he was born.

Gran Teatre del Liceu

Built in 1847, destroyed by fire in 1994, and resurrected five years later, Barcelona's grand operatic stage, the **Gran Teatre del Liceu** (📞93 485 99 00; www.liceubarcelona.cat; La Rambla 51-59; tour 50min/25min €16/6; 🕐50min tour 9.30am & 10.30am, 25min tour schedule varies; Ⓜ Liceu) launched the careers of José Carreras and Montserrat Caballé. The marble staircase, Saló dels Miralls (Hall of Mirrors) and 19th-century stalls are original.

Plaça Reial

One of the loveliest squares in all of Barcelona, Plaça Reial is where many visitors divert from La Rambla and enter the city's Gothic Quarter, which shadows La Rambla from start to finish. A nightlife hub, popular meeting point and home to some modest early Gaudí structures, the square is a place you'll want to linger.

Centre d'Art Santa Mònica

Further south La Rambla gets seedier, widens out and changes its name to La Rambla de Santa Mònica. This stretch is named after the Convent de Santa Mònica, a monastery converted into an art gallery and cultural centre, the **Centre d'Art Santa Mònica** (📞93 567 11 10; www.artssantamonica.gencat.cat; La Rambla 7; admission free; 🕐11am-9pm Tue-Sat, 11am-5pm Sun; Ⓜ Drassanes).

Museu de Cera

In a lane off La Rambla's eastern side, Barcelona's wax museum **Museu de Cera** (📞93 317 26 49; www.museocerabcn. com; Passatge de la Banca 7; adult/concession/under 4 €15/9/free; 🕐10am-10pm summer, 10am-1.30pm & 4-7.30pm Mon-Fri, 11am-2pm & 4.30-8.30pm Sat & Sun winter; Ⓜ Drassanes)

Mercat de la Boqueria

has more than 300 wax figures of familiar faces from around the world. There's everything from displays of twisted medieval torture to likenesses of Prince Charles and Camilla.

Mirador de Colom

Centuries after he stumbled across the Americas, Columbus (Colón in Spanish, Colom in Catalan) was honoured with the **Mirador de Colom** (📞93 302 52 24; www.barcelonaturisme.com; Plaça del Portal de la Pau; adult/concession €6/4; 🕐8.30am-8.30pm summer, 8.30am-7.30pm winter; Ⓜ Drassanes), a 60m-high monument built for the Universal Exposition in 1888. Catch a lift to the top for a fine view down La Rambla.

Top Sights
La Catedral

Barcelona's central place of worship presents a magnificent image. The richly decorated main facade, laced with gargoyles and the stone intricacies you would expect of northern European Gothic, sets it quite apart from other churches in Barcelona. The facade was actually added in 1870, although the rest of the building was built between 1298 and 1460.

👁 Map p32, C3

www.catedralbcn.org

Plaça de la Seu

admission free, 'donation entrance' €7, choir €3, roof €3

🕑 8am-12.45pm & 5.15-7.30pm Mon-Fri, to 8pm Sat & Sun, 'donation entrance' 1-5pm Mon-Sat, 2-5pm Sun

Ⓜ Jaume I

Interior view, La Catedral

Don't Miss

The Design

The interior is a broad, soaring space divided into a central nave and two aisles by lines of elegant, slim pillars. The cathedral was one of the few churches in Barcelona spared by the anarchists in the civil war, so its ornamentation, never overly lavish, is intact.

Coro

In the middle of the central nave is the late 14th-century, exquisitely sculpted timber *coro* (choir stalls). The coats of arms on the stalls belong to members of the Barcelona chapter of the Order of the Golden Fleece.

Crypt

Beneath the main altar, the crypt contains the tomb of Santa Eulàlia. One of Barcelona's patron saints, she was martyred by the pagan Romans. The tomb depicts some of the gruesome tortures she suffered.

The Roof

For a bird's-eye view of medieval Barcelona, visit the cathedral's roof and tower by taking the lift (€3) from the Capella de les Animes del Purgatori near the northeast transept.

Claustre

From the southwest transept, exit to the leafy *claustre* (cloister), with its fountains and flock of 13 geese. The geese supposedly represent the age of Santa Eulàlia at the time of her martyrdom and have, generation after generation, been squawking here since medieval days. One of the chapels commemorates 930 priests, monks and nuns martyred in the Spanish Civil War.

☑ **Top Tips**

▶ It is worth paying for the 'donation entrance' to avoid the crowds and appreciate the splendour of the building in relative peace.

▶ If you're around at 6pm on Saturday or 11am on Sunday, check out the *sardana* (Catalan national dance) performances in the square in front of the cathedral.

✕ **Take a Break**

Head to the Carrer dels Banys Nous for a fortifying cone of churros – deep-fried dough sticks – at **Xurreria** (Map p32, C4; ☎ 93 318 76 91; Carrer dels Banys Nous 8; cone €1.20; ☻ 7.30am-1.30pm & 3.30-8.15pm; Ⓜ Jaume I).

A couple of minutes' walk away, **Els Quatre Gats** (Map p32, B1; ☎ 93 302 41 40; www.4gats.com; Carrer de Montsió 3; mains €21-29; ☻ 12.30-4.30pm & 6.30pm-1am; 🛜; Ⓜ Urquinaona) makes for an architecturally splendid pit stop.

Local Life
A Barri Gòtic Sunday

The Barri Gòtic can seem overrun by visitors at times, but it's on Sunday more than any other day that locals reclaim their neighbourhood, colonising the squares with small markets and frequenting places little known to out-of-town visitors. Sunday is also the only day when the town hall – a Catalan icon – throws open its doors.

❶ Spiritual Start

Sunday mass remains an important part of life in the Barri Gòtic, so where better to begin than the 14th-century **Església de Sants Just i Pastor** (📞93 301 74 33; www.basilicasantjust.cat; Plaça de Sant Just; ⏱11am-2pm & 5-9pm Mon-Sat, 10am-1pm Sun; Ⓜ Liceu or Jaume I)? This Gothic church holds a special place in Catalan hearts: on 11 September 1924, Gaudí was arrested here for refusing to speak Spanish to a policeman.

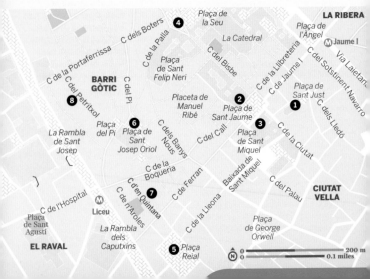

❷ Catalan Power

On Plaça de Sant Jaume, the **Palau de la Generalitat** (www.president.cat; ⏰2nd & 4th weekend of month; Ⓜ Jaume I), the seat of Catalonia's regional government, was adapted from several Gothic mansions. The Saló de Sant Jordi (Hall of St George) is typical of the sumptuous interior. Visits must be booked online.

❸ Town Hall Tour

Barcelona's **Ajuntament** (Casa de la Ciutat; ☎93 402 70 00; www.barcelonaturisme.com; Plaça de Sant Jaume; admission free; ⏰10.30am-1.30pm Sun; Ⓜ Jaume I) has been the seat of city power since the 14th century. It has a Catalan Gothic side facade, while its spectacular interior features a majestic staircase and the splendidly restored Saló de Cent (Chamber of the One Hundred).

❹ Sardana

Catching a performance of *sardana*, the Catalan folk dance par excellence, is always a memorable event, at once an enjoyable spectacle and an important reassertion of Catalan identity. Your best chance is to turn up to **Plaça Nova**, next to La Catedral, at 11am on Sundays (or 6pm on Saturdays), when performances usually take place.

❺ Coins & Stamps

While much of Barcelona is still sleeping off the excesses of the night before, dedicated collectors make their way to the **Coin & Stamp Market** (Mercat de Numismàtica i Filatèlia; Plaça Reial; ⏰9am-2.30pm Sun; Ⓜ Liceu). Like all flea markets, it's always worth leafing through what's on offer in search of treasure, while some stallholders have branched out to sell a range of knick-knacks, both antique and otherwise.

❻ Art & Crafts Market

On one of the Barri Gòtic's prettiest little squares, you'll find dozens of local artists and artisans showcasing their work in this lively **crafts market** (Mostra d'Art; Plaça de Sant Josep Oriol; ⏰11am-8.30pm Sat, 10am-3pm Sun; Ⓜ Liceu). It happens on Plaça de Sant Josep Oriol, which is named after the 17th-century parish priest (canonised in 1909) based in the church here.

❼ Sunday Lunch

Founded in 1786, **Can Culleretes** (☎93 317 30 22; www.culleretes.com; Carrer Quintana 5; mains €10-17; ⏰1.30-4pm & 9-11pm Tue-Sat, 1.30-4pm Sun; Ⓜ Liceu) is still going strong, with crowds flocking to enjoy its rambling interior, old-fashioned tile-filled decor, and enormous helpings of traditional Catalan food.

❽ Chocolate con Churros

An afternoon favourite for *barcelonins*, **Granja La Pallaresa** (☎93 302 20 36; Carrer del Petritxol 11; ⏰9am-1pm daily, plus 4-9pm Mon, Sat & Sun; Ⓜ Liceu) serves up thick and rich hot chocolate. Order some crispy churros (*xurros* in Catalan; deep-fried dough strips) for some delectable dunking.

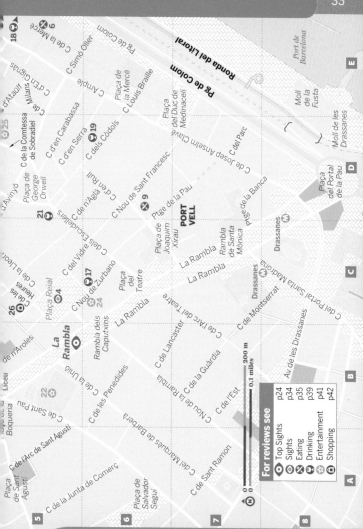

Sights

Museu d'Història de Barcelona

MUSEUM

1 Map p32, D3

One of Barcelona's most fascinating museums takes you back through the centuries to the very foundations of Roman Barcino. You'll stroll over ruins of the old streets, sewers, laundries and wine- and fish-making factories that flourished here following the town's founding by Emperor Augustus around 10 BC. Equally impressive is the building itself, which was once part of the Palau Reial Major (Grand Royal Palace) on Plaça del Rei, among the key locations of medieval princely power in Barcelona. (MUHBA; ☑ 93 256 21 00; www.museuhistoria.bcn.cat; Plaça del Rei; adult/concession/child €7/5/free, 3-8pm Sun & 1st Sun of month free; ⊙10am-7pm Tue-Sat, 10am-8pm Sun; Ⓜ Jaume I)

Museu Frederic Marès

MUSEUM

2 Map p32, C2

One of the wildest collections of historical curios lies inside this vast medieval complex, once part of the royal palace of the counts of Barcelona. A rather worn coat of arms on the wall indicates that it was also, for a while, the seat of the Spanish Inquisition in Barcelona. Frederic Marès i Deulovol (1893–1991) was a rich sculptor, traveller and obsessive collector, and displays of religious art and vast varieties of bric-a-brac litter the museum. (☑ 93 256 35 00; www.

museumares.bcn.cat; Plaça de Sant Iu 5; adult/concession/child €4.20/2.40/free, after 3pm Sun & 1st Sun of month free; ⊙10am-7pm Tue-Sat, 11am-8pm Sun; Ⓜ Jaume I)

Temple Romà d'August

RUIN

3 Map p32, D3

Opposite the southeast end of La Catedral, narrow Carrer del Paradis leads towards Plaça de Sant Jaume. Inside No 10, an intriguing building with Gothic and baroque touches, are four columns and the architrave of Barcelona's main Roman temple, dedicated to Caesar Augustus and built to worship his imperial highness in the 1st century AD. (☑ 93 256 21 22; Carrer del Paradis 10; admission free; ⊙10am-2pm Mon, to 7pm Tue-Sat, to 8pm Sun; Ⓜ Jaume I)

Plaça Reial

SQUARE

4 Map p32, C5

One of the most photogenic squares in Barcelona, Plaça Reial is a delightful retreat from the traffic and pedestrian mobs on nearby La Rambla. Numerous eateries, bars and nightspots lie beneath the arcades of 19th-century neoclassical buildings, with a buzz of activity at all hours. (ⓂLiceu)

Església de Santa Maria del Pi

CHURCH

5 Map p32, B4

This striking 14th-century church is a classic of Catalan Gothic, with an imposing facade, a wide interior and a single nave. The simple decor in the

Outdoor dining, Plaça Reial

main sanctuary contrasts with the gilded chapels and exquisite stained-glass windows that bathe the interior in ethereal light. The beautiful rose window above its entrance is one of the world's largest. Occasional concerts are staged here (classical guitar, choral groups and chamber orchestras). (📞93 318 47 43; www.basilicadelpi.com; Plaça del Pi; adult/concession/under 6 €4/3/free; ⏱10am-6pm; Ⓜ Liceu)

Eating

La Plata   TAPAS €

6 🍽 Map p32, E5

Tucked away on a narrow lane near the waterfront, La Plata is a humble but well-loved bodega that serves just three plates: *pescadito frito* (small fried fish), *butifarra* (sausage) and tomato salad. Add in the drinkable, affordable wines (€1.10 per glass) and you have the makings of a fine pre-dinner tapas spot. (📞93 315 10 09; www.barlaplata.com; Carrer de la Mercè 28; tapas €2.50-5; ⏱9am-3.30pm & 6.30-11.30pm Mon-Sat; Ⓜ Jaume I)

La Vinateria del Call   SPANISH €€

7 🍽 Map p32, C3

In a magical setting in the former Jewish quarter, this tiny jewel box of a restaurant (recently extended to add another dining room) serves up tasty Iberian dishes including Galician

Top Tip

Roman Walls

The city's first architects of note were the Romans, who built a town here in the 1st century BC. Large relics of its 3rd- and 4th-century walls can still be seen in the Barri Gòtic, particularly at Plaça de Ramon Berenguer el Gran and by the northern end of Carrer del Sotstinent Navarro.

octopus, cider-cooked chorizo and the Catalan *escalivada* (roasted peppers, aubergine and onions) with anchovies. Portions are small and made for sharing, and there's a good and affordable selection of wines. (☎93 302 60 92; www.lavinateriadelcall.com; Carrer de Sant Domènec del Call 9; small plates €7-12; ⏰7.30pm-1am; Ⓜ Jaume I)

Cafè de l'Acadèmia
CATALAN €€

 8   Map p32, D3

Expect a mix of traditional Catalan dishes with the occasional creative twist. At lunchtime, local Ajuntament (town hall) office workers pounce on the *menú del día* (daily set menu; €14.30). In the evening it is rather more romantic, as low lighting emphasises the intimacy of the beamed ceiling and stone walls. On warm days you can also dine on the pretty square at the front. (☎93 319 82 53; Carrer dels Lledó 1; mains €14-18; ⏰1-3.30pm & 8-11pm Mon-Fri; 🛜; Ⓜ Jaume I)

Federal
CAFE €€

9   Map p32, D6

Don't be intimidated by the industrial chic, the sea of open MacBooks or the stack of design mags – this branch of the Poble Sec Federal mothership is incredibly welcoming, with healthy, hearty and good-value food. Choose a salad and a topping (poached eggs, strips of chicken) or a yellow curry, say, and follow it up with a moist slab of carrot cake. (☎93 280 81 71; www. federalcafe.es; Passatge de la Pau 11; mains €9-12; ⏰9am-midnight Mon-Thu, to 1am Fri & Sat, 9am-5.30pm Sun; 🛜; Ⓜ Drassanes)

Belmonte
TAPAS €€

 10   Map p32, E5

This tiny tapas joint in the southern reaches of the Barri Gòtic whips up beautifully prepared small plates – including an excellent *truita* (tortilla), rich *patatons a la sal* (salted new potatoes with romesco sauce) and tender *carpaccio de pop* (octopus carpaccio). Wash it down with the housemade *vermut* (vermouth). (☎93 310 76 84; Carrer de la Mercè 29; tapas €4-10, mains €12; ⏰8pm-midnight Tue-Sat, plus 1-3.30pm Sat; 🛜; Ⓜ Jaume I)

Rasoterra
VEGETARIAN €€

11   Map p32, D4

A delightful addition to the Barri Gòtic, Rasoterra cooks up first-rate vegetarian dishes in a Zen-like setting with tall ceilings, low-playing jazz and fresh flowers on the tables. The

Understand

Growth of a City

The Romans were, in the 1st century BC, the first to build a lasting settlement on the plain where Barcelona now sprawls. The nucleus of their city, known as Barcino, lay within defensive walls whose outline roughly traced what is now the Barri Gòtic, a more or less standard rectangular Roman town. The forum lay approximately where Plaça de Sant Jaume is now and the whole city covered little more than 10 hectares.

In the centuries that followed, settlements spread beyond the city walls. By the 13th and 14th centuries, Barcelona was the capital of an expanding Mediterranean empire with a rapidly growing population. Its walls were pushed outwards to enclose what we now know as El Raval and La Ribera; La Rambla (which takes its name from a seasonal stream, or *raml* in Arabic) lay outside the city walls until the 14th century.

By the mid-19th century, Barcelona was again bursting at the seams. The road between Barcelona and the then village of Gràcia was lined with trees in the 1820s, giving birth to Passeig de Gràcia with gardens and fields on either side. The medieval walls were knocked down by 1856, and in 1869 work began on L'Eixample (the Extension, or Enlargement) to fill the open country between Barcelona and Gràcia.

Designed by Ildefons Cerdà, L'Eixample took the form of a grid with diamond-shaped intersections, broken up with gardens and parks and grafted onto the northern edge of the old town, starting at what is now Plaça de Catalunya.

The plan was revolutionary; until then it had been illegal to build on the plains, the area being a military zone. Construction continued well into the 20th century. Well-to-do families snapped up prime plots and raised fanciful buildings in the eclectic style of the Modernistas. With restrictions no longer in place, Barcelona grew exponentially, swallowing up towns such as Gràcia, Sant Martí, Sants and Sant Andreu.

Top Tip

Menú del Día

One great way to cap prices on weekday lunches is to order the *menú del día*, which usually costs around €10 to €15. You'll be given a menu with five or six starters, the same number of mains and a handful of desserts – choose one of each.

creative, globally influenced menu changes regularly and might feature Vietnamese-style coconut pancakes with tofu and vegetables, beluga lentils with basmati rice, and pear and goat cheese quesadillas. Good vegan and gluten-free options. (📞93 318 69 26; www.rasoterra.cat; Carrer del Palau 5; mains €13; ☺7-11pm Tue, 1-4pm & 7-11pm Wed-Sun; 🛜🥦; Ⓜ Jaume I)

Onofre   SPANISH €€

12 🍴 Map p32, B1

Famed for its (good, affordable) wine selections, Onofre is a small, modern eatery (and wine shop and delicatessen) that has a strong local following for its delicious tapas and great-value lunch specials (three-course *prix fixé* for €10.75, or €14.75 on Saturdays). Among the delectable tapas selections: Italian greens with foie shavings, duck confit, codfish carpaccio and oven-baked prawns. (📞93 317 69 37; www.onofre.net; Carrer de les Magdalenes 19; mains

€9-14; ☺10am-4pm & 7.30pm-midnight Mon-Sat; 🛜; Ⓜ Jaume I)

Koy Shunka   JAPANESE €€€

13 🍴 Map p32, C1

Down a narrow lane north of the cathedral, Koy Shunka opens a portal to exquisite dishes from the East – mouth-watering sushi, sashimi, seared Wagyu beef and flavour-rich seaweed salads are served alongside inventive cooked fusion dishes like steamed clams with sake or tempura of scallops and king prawns with Japanese mushrooms. Don't miss the house specialty of tender *toro* (tuna belly). (📞93 412 79 39; www.koyshunka.com; Carrer de Copons 7; multicourse menu €82-128; ☺1.30-3pm & 8.30-11pm Tue-Sat, 1.30-3pm Sun; Ⓜ Urquinaona)

Pla   FUSION €€€

14 🍴 Map p32, D4

One of Gòtic's long-standing favourites, Pla is a stylish, romantically lit medieval dining room where the cooks churn out such temptations as oxtail braised in red wine, seared tuna with oven-roasted peppers, and polenta with seasonal mushrooms. It has a tasting menu for €52 Sunday to Thursday. (📞93 412 65 52; www.restaurantpla.cat; Carrer de la Bellafila 5; mains €17-23; ☺7-11.30pm Sun-Thu, to midnight Fri & Sat; Ⓜ Jaume I)

RAFAEL ELIAS/GETTY IMAGES ©

Evening cocktails

Drinking

Ginger
COCKTAIL BAR

15 Map p32, D3

Tucked away just off peaceful Plaça de Sant Just, Ginger is an art-deco-style multilevel drinking den with low lighting, finely crafted cocktails and good ambient sounds (provided by vinyl-spinning DJs some nights). It's a mellow spot that's great for sipping wine and sampling from the gourmet tapas menu. (☑93 310 53 09; www. ginger.cat; Carrer de Palma de Sant Just 1; ☺7.30pm-2.30am Tue-Thu, 7.30pm-3am Fri & Sat; Ⓜ Jaume I)

L'Ascensor
BAR

16 Map p32, D4

Named after the lift (elevator) doors that serve as the front door, this elegant drinking den with its vaulted brick ceilings, vintage mirrors and marble-topped bar gathers a faithful crowd that comes for old-fashioned cocktails and lively conversation against a soundtrack of up-tempo jazz and funk. (☑93 318 53 47; Carrer de la Bellafila 3; ☺6pm-2.30am Sun-Thu, to 3am Fri & Sat; ☜; Ⓜ Jaume I)

Barri Gòtic Cafes

Local Life

Some of Barcelona's most atmospheric cafes lie hidden in the old cobbled lanes of the Barri Gòtic. **Salterio** (Map p32, C4; Carrer de Sant Domènec del Call 4; ⏱11am-midnight, to 1am Fri & Sat; 🛜; Ⓜ Jaume I) serves teas and *sardo* (grilled flatbread pizzas) amid stone walls and ambient Middle Eastern music. Nearby, **Čaj Chai** (Map p32, C4; ☎93 301 95 92; www.cajchai.com; Carrer de Sant Domènec del Call 12; ⏱10.30am-10pm; Ⓜ Jaume I) is a bright and buzzing tearoom with numerous teas on offer. Famed for its heavenly desserts, **Caelum** (Map p32, B3; ☎93 302 69 93; www.caelumbarcelona.com; Carrer de la Palla 8; ⏱10.30am-8.30pm Mon-Thu, to 11pm Fri & Sat, to 9pm Sun; Ⓜ Liceu) has a dainty upstairs cafe as well as an underground chamber with medieval stone walls and flickering candles.

Ocaña
BAR

17   Map p32, C6

Named after a flamboyant artist who once lived on Plaça Reial, Ocaña is a beautifully designed space with chandeliers and plush furnishings. Have a seat on the terrace and watch the passing people parade, or head downstairs to the Moorish-inspired Apotheke bar or the chic lounge a few steps away, where DJs spin for a mix of beauties and bohemians on weekend nights. (☎93 676 48 14; www.ocana.cat; Plaça Reial 13; ⏱noon-2.30am Mon-Fri, 11am-2.30am Sat & Sun; 🛜; Ⓜ Liceu)

Sor Rita
BAR

18   Map p32, E5

A lover of all things kitsch, Sor Rita is pure eye candy, from its leopard-print wallpaper to its high-heel-festooned ceiling and deliciously irreverent decorations inspired by the films of Pedro Almodóvar. It's a fun and festive scene, with special-event nights including tarot readings on Mondays, €5 all-you-can-eat snack buffets on Tuesdays, karaoke or cabaret on Wednesdays, and gin specials on Thursdays. (☎93 176 62 66; www.sorritabar.es; Carrer de la Mercè 27; ⏱7pm-3am Sun-Thu, to 3.30am Fri & Sat; 🛜; Ⓜ Jaume I)

Polaroid
BAR

19   Map p32, D6

For a dash of 1980s nostalgia, Polaroid is a blast from the past, with its wall-mounted VHS tapes, old film posters, comic-book-covered tables, action-figure displays and other kitschy decor. Not surprisingly, it draws a fun, unpretentious crowd who comes for cheap *cañas* (draught beer), mojitos and free popcorn. (☎93 186 66 69; www.polaroidbar.es; Carrer dels Còdols 29; ⏱7pm-2.30am Sun-Thu, to 3am Fri & Sat; Ⓜ Drassanes)

La Cerveteca
BAR

20   Map p32, E4

An unmissable stop for beer lovers, La Cerveteca serves an impressive variety of global craft brews. In addition to scores of bottled beers, there's a frequent rotation of what's on draught.

Gran Teatre del Liceu

Cheeses, *jamón ibérico* and other charcuterie selections are on hand, including *cecina* (cured horse meat). (www.lacerveteca.com; Carrer d'en Gignàs 25; ⏰6pm-midnight Tue-Fri, noon-3.30pm & 6pm-midnight Sat, noon-3.30pm Sun; Ⓜ Jaume I)

Marula Café   BAR

 21 Map p32, D5

A fantastic find in the heart of the Barri Gòtic, Marula will transport you to the 1970s and the best in funk and soul. James Brown fans will think they've died and gone to heaven. It's not, however, a monothematic place and DJs slip in other tunes, from breakbeat to house. Samba and other Brazilian dance sounds also penetrate here. (🕿93 318 76 90; www.marulacafe.com; Carrer dels Escudellers 49; ⏰11pm-6am Wed-Sun; Ⓜ Liceu)

Entertainment

Gran Teatre del Liceu   THEATRE, LIVE MUSIC

22 ⭐ Map p32, B5

Barcelona's grand old opera house, restored after a fire in 1994, is one of the most technologically advanced theatres in the world. To take a seat in the grand auditorium, returned to all its 19th-century glory but with the very latest in acoustics, is to be transported to another age. (☏93 485 99 00; www.liceubarcelona.com; La Rambla 51-59; ⊗box office 9.30am-8pm Mon-Fri, 9.30am-6pm Sat & Sun; Ⓜ Liceu)

El Paraigua
LIVE MUSIC

23 ⭐ Map p32, C4

A tiny chocolate box of dark tinted Modernisme, the 'Umbrella' has been serving up drinks since the 1960s. The turn-of-the-20th-century decor was transferred here from a shop knocked down elsewhere in the district and cobbled back together to create this cosy locale. (☏93 302 11 31; www.elparaigua.com; Carrer del Pas de l'Ensenyança 2; ⊗noon-midnight Sun-Wed, to 2am Thu, to 3am Fri & Sat; Ⓜ Liceu)

Jamboree
LIVE MUSIC

24 ⭐ Map p32, C6

For over half a century, Jamboree has been bringing joy to the jivers of Barcelona, with high-calibre acts featuring jazz trios, blues, Afrobeats, Latin sounds and big-band sounds. Two concerts are held most nights (at 8pm and 10pm), after which Jamboree morphs into a DJ-spinning club at midnight. WTF jam sessions are held Mondays (entrance a mere €5). (☏93 319 17 89; www.masimas.com/jamboree; Plaça Reial 17; €12-20; ⊗8pm-6am; Ⓜ Liceu)

Harlem Jazz Club
JAZZ

25 ⭐ Map p32, D5

This narrow, old-city dive is one of the best spots in town for jazz, as well as funk, Latin, blues and gypsy jazz. It attracts a mixed crowd who maintains a respectful silence during the acts. Most concerts start around 10pm. Get in early if you want a seat in front of the stage. (☏93 310 07 55; www.harlemjazzclub.es; Carrer de la Comtessa de Sobradiel 8; €6-10; ⊗10.30pm-3am Sun & Tue-Thu, to 5am Fri & Sat; Ⓜ Liceu)

Shopping

Herboristeria del Rei
BEAUTY

26 🔒 Map p32, C5

Once patronised by Queen Isabel II, this timeless corner store flogs all sorts of weird and wonderful herbs, spices and medicinal plants. It's doing so since 1823 and the decor has barely changed since the 1860s. However, some of the products have, and you'll find anything from fragrant soaps to massage oil nowadays. (☏93 318 05 12; www.herboristeriadelrei.com; Carrer del Vidre 1; ⊗2-8.30pm Mon, 10am-8.30pm Tue-Sat; Ⓜ Liceu)

Artesania Catalunya
HANDICRAFTS

27 🔒 Map p32, C4

A celebration of Catalan products, this nicely designed store is a great place to browse for unique gifts. You'll find jewellery with designs inspired by

La Rambla (p24)

Roman iconography (as well as works that reference Gaudí and Barcelona's Gothic era), plus pottery, wooden toys, silk scarves, notebooks, housewares and more. (☏ 93 342 75 20; www.bcncrafts. com; Carrer dels Banys Nous 11; ⊙ 10am-8pm Mon-Sat, to 2pm Sun; Ⓜ Liceu)

Taller de Marionetas Travi
MARIONETTES

28 🔒 Map p32, B1

Opened in the 1970s, this atmospheric shop sells beautifully handcrafted marionettes. Don Quixote, Sancho and other iconic Spanish figures are on hand, as well as unusual works from other parts of the world – including rare Sicilian puppets and pieces from Myanmar (Burma), Indonesia and elsewhere. (☏ 93 412 66 92; www.marionetas travi.com; Carrer de n'Amargós 4; ⊙ noon-8pm Mon-Sat; Ⓜ Urquinaona)

La Manual Alpargatera
SHOES

29 🔒 Map p32, C4

Clients from Salvador Dalí to Jean Paul Gaultier have ordered a pair of espadrilles (rope-soled canvas shoes) from this famous store. The shop was founded just after the Spanish Civil War, though the roots of the simple shoe design date back hundreds of years and originated in the Catalan Pyrenees. (☏ 93 301 01 72; www.lamanualalpargatera.es; Carrer d'Avinyó 7; ⊙ 9.30am-1.30pm & 4.30-8pm Mon-Fri, from 10am Sat; Ⓜ Liceu)

Explore

El Raval

Long one of the most rough-and-tumble parts of Barcelona, El Raval is now undeniably hip in a grungy, inner-city way. Attractions here include the Mercat de la Boqueria, two stunning centres for contemporary arts, and lively streets dotted with colourful shops, eateries and cafes. Night-time is El Raval's forte, with its mix of eccentric, trendy and downright ancient bars and clubs.

The Sights in a Day

☀ The **Mercat de la Boqueria** (p46) ranks among the most enduring of Barcelona institutions and it's at its best in the morning. Leave behind the cries of fishmongers and make your way to the **MACBA** (p51) to sample the cutting edge of contemporary art.

☀ After a lunch of regionally sourced delicacies at buzzing **Mam i Teca** (p52), take in an exhibition or two at the **Centre de Cultura Contemporània de Barcelona** (p51). Head south, via Barcelona's favourite milk bar, **Granja M Viader** (p49), to the old city's only Gaudí masterpiece, **Palau Güell** (p51), then continue on to **Església de Sant Pau del Camp** (p52), one of Barcelona's most tranquil churches.

☾ Start off the evening with a show at **Jazz Sí Club** (p49), followed by dinner at celebrated **Suculent** (p53). Afterwards take in El Raval's nightlife at vintage drinking spots like **Bar Marsella** (pictured left; p49) or **La Confitería** (p53).

For a local's day in El Raval, see p48.

 Top Sights

Mercat de la Boqueria (p46)

 Local Life

Revelling in El Raval (p48)

💜 **Best of Barcelona**

Art & Architecture

MACBA (p51)

Centre de Cultura Contemporània de Barcelona (p51)

Palau Güell (p51)

Catalan Cooking

Suculent (p53)

Mam i Teca (p52)

Mercat de la Boqueria (p46)

Elisabets (p49)

Getting There

Ⓜ **Metro** Your best transport option. Catalunya (lines 1, 3, 6 and 7) and Universitat (lines 1 and 2) sit at the neighbourhood's northern end, while Liceu (line 3) occupies the midpoint, on La Rambla to the east.

Ⓜ **Metro** Drassanes (line 3), Paral·lel (lines 2 and 3) and Sant Antoni (line 2) are good for southern El Raval.

Top Sights
Mercat de la Boqueria

Barcelona's most agreeable sensory experience is found at its central market. Completed in 1914 with a Modernisme-influenced design, this is one Barcelona landmark where the architecture is overshadowed by what lies within – the freshest produce from around Spain, the evocative starting point of many a memorable Barcelona meal, and a hum of activity unlike anywhere else in the city. Wander to get lost. Marvel at the sheer variety. And then sit back to watch from a bar stool.

👁 Map p50, C3

📞 93 412 13 15

www.boqueria.info

La Rambla 91

🕙 8am-8.30pm Mon-Sat

Ⓜ Liceu

Don't Miss

Fish Market

While stalls aimed at tourists make tentative inroads, the fish market in the market's geographical centre is the guardian of tradition. Razor clams and red prawns, salmon, sea bass and swordfish, it's all as fresh as when it was caught; so much so that there's scarcely a fishy aroma to inhale. Barcelona's love affair with fish and seafood starts here.

Juanito at Bar Pinotxo

As one respected Barcelona food critic described him, Juanito is 'the true spirit of the market'. Head barman at **Bar Pinotxo** (www.pinotxobar.com; mains €8-17; ⊙6am-4pm Mon-Sat; Ⓜ Liceu) for more than four decades, resplendent in waistcoat and bowtie, and unfailingly warm in many languages and none, he cajoles his staff, greets passers-by and announces the daily specials in the finest Barcelona tradition of food as performance.

El Llar del Pernil

The family-run **Joan La Llar del Pernil** (☏93 317 95 29; Stalls 667, 669, 670 & 671, ⊙8am-3pm Mon-Thu, to 8pm Fri & Sat; Ⓜ Liceu) is our pick of the numerous purveyors of *jamón* (cured Spanish-style ham; *pernil* in Catalan) scattered around the market. Stall owner Joan knows his *jamón*, cheerfully regaling passers-by with lessons in the dark arts of cured meats as he cuts another wafer-thin slice and hands it over to try.

El Quim

The food at **El Quim** (☏93 301 98 10; www.elquim delaboqueria.com; ⊙7am-4pm Tue-Thu, to 5pm Fri & Sat; Ⓜ Liceu), buried in the heart of the market, is as fresh as the market produce. It offers a dazzling array of dishes, but does particularly wonderful things with eggs: *tortilla de patatas* (Spanish omelette), fried eggs with squid, or with foie gras... Pull up a stool.

☑ Top Tips

▶ The market is closed on Sunday.

▶ Many stalls, including most of those selling fish, are closed on Monday.

▶ The market's stallholders are among the world's most photographed – ask permission before taking pictures and where possible buy something from their stall.

▶ Gather food from your favourite stalls with a picnic in mind – having a foodie purpose brings a whole new dimension to your market experience.

✗ Take a Break

For market-fresh food and some of the market's best cooking, pull up a stool at El Quim.

To soak up the clamour from a front-row vantage point, stop by Bar Pinotxo.

Local Life
Revelling in El Raval

El Raval is a neighbourhood whose contradictory impulses are legion. This journey through the local life of the *barrio* takes you from haunts beloved by the savvy young professionals moving into the area to gritty streetscapes and one-time slums frequented by Barcelona's immigrants and street-walkers. En route, we stop at places that, unlike the rest of the neighbourhood, haven't changed in decades.

❶ A Neighbourhood Square

For a slice of local life, Plaça de Vincenç Martorell is difficult to beat. It's where the locals come to play with their kids or read the newspapers over a coffee or wine at **Bar Kasparo** (Plaça de Vicenç Martorell 4; ⏰9am-11pm; Ⓜ Catalunya). Just a short hop from La Rambla, this is Barcelona as locals live it.

2 Musical Browsing

Carrer dels Tallers was once lined with music shops. Sadly, the economic crisis took its toll and now only **Discos Castelló** (Carrer dels Tallers 7; ⏱10am-8.30pm Mon-Sat; MCatalunya) remains, selling new and secondhand CDs and vinyl of all types, along with a selection of related books and paraphernalia.

3 Home-Style Cooking

Northern El Raval is rapidly gentrifying, but places like **Elisabets** (📞93 317 58 26; Carrer d'Elisabets 2-4; mains €8-10, menú del día €10.85; ⏱7.30am-11.30pm Mon-Sat Sep-Jul; MCatalunya) hold firm. The walls are lined with old radio sets and the lunch menu varies daily. If you prefer à la carte, try the *ragú de jabalí* (wild boar stew) and finish with *mel i mató* (a Catalan dessert made from cheese and honey).

4 Homemade Hot Chocolate

The fifth generation of its founding family runs **Granja M Viader** (📞93 318 34 86; www.granjaviader.cat; Carrer d'en Xuclà 6; ⏱9am-1.30pm & 5-9pm Mon-Sat; MLiceu), an atmospheric milk bar and cafe established in 1873. This place invented *cacaolat*, the chocolate-and-skimmed-milk drink now popular all over Spain. Try a cup of homemade hot chocolate and whipped cream (ask for a *suís*).

5 Preloved Shopping

Looking for fashion bargains that are perfect for passing unnoticed in this 'hood? In little more than 100m along Carrer de la Riera Baixa, from Carrer del Carme to Carrer de l'Hospital, you'll find nearly a dozen clothes shops, mostly selling secondhand.

6 Live Music

Run by the Taller de Músics (Musicians' Workshop), the tiny **Jazz Sí Club** (📞93 329 00 20; www.tallerdemusics. com; Carrer de Requesens 2; €4-10, incl drink; ⏱8.30-11pm Tue-Sat, 6.30-10pm Sun; MSant Antoni) hosts a varied line-up, from jazz jams through to some good flamenco (Friday nights). Thursday night is Cuban night. Concerts start around 8.30pm or so, but arrive early to get a good spot.

7 Scenic Stroll

For a wide cross-section of the neighbourhood's multicultural mix, take a stroll down the palm-lined Rambla del Raval. Flanked by restaurants and outdoor cafes, this promenade is Barcelona's newest *rambla* (laid out in 1995). Don't miss the enormous, whiskered Gat (Cat) sculpture by Colombian artist Fernando Botero, a favourite meeting spot in El Raval.

8 Late-Night Drinks

End the day at **Bar Marsella** (📞93 442 72 63; Carrer de Sant Pau 65; ⏱10pm-2.30am Mon-Thu, 10pm-3am Fri & Sat; MLiceu), which opened in 1820 and has barely changed since; assorted chandeliers, tiles and mirrors decorate its one rambunctious room. As in Hemingway's time, absinthe is the drink of choice, which should give you a warm glow – though treat this potent libation with respect!

Universitat de Barcelona

Gran Via de les Corts Catalanes

Ronda de la Universitat

Plaça de la Universitat

Universitat

C de Pelai

C dels Tallers

Centre de Cultura Contemporània de Barcelona

MACBA

Plaça dels Àngels

Plaça de Terenci Moix

C de Valldonzella

C del Tigre

C del Lleó

C de Joaquín Costa

Montalegre

C dels Àngels

Plaça del Pes de la Palla

Ronda de Sant Antoni

C de la Lluna

C de la Riera Alta

Plaça del Pedró

C del Carme

C de l'Hospital

Sant Antoni

Ronda de Sant Pau

C de la Cera

C de l'Aurora

C de les Carretes

C de les Carretes

C de la Riereta

C de la Reina Amàlia

SANT ANTONI

Plaça de Josep Maria Folch i Torres

Rambla del Raval

Plaça de Salvador Seguí

Església de Sant Pau del Camp

C de les Tàpies

C Nou de la Rambla

Av del Paral·lel

Paral·lel

Parc de les Tres Xemeneies

Catalunya

Plaça de Catalunya

Turisme de Barcelona

C de Fontanella

C de Bergara

Catalunya

Rambla de Canaletes

Plaça de Vicenç Martorell

C del Notariat

Rambla dels Estudis

C de Santa Anna

C de la Canuda

Rambla de la Vila de Madrid

C de Montsió

C Comtal

Urquinaona

Via Laietana

LA RIBERA

Plaça d'Antoni Maura

C de la Portaferrissa

Rambla de Sant Josep

Mercat de la Boqueria

Liceu

C de la Boqueria

Rambla de Sant Josep

Plaça de Sant Josep Oriol

BARRI GÒTIC

Plaça Nova

Plaça de la Seu

C de la Palla

C del Bisbe

Plaça de Sant Jaume

C del Call

CIUTAT VELLA

C d'Aviny

Plaça Reial

C de Ferran

La Rambla

C de Sant Pau

C de la Junta de Comerç

C del Marquès de Barberà

Palau Güell

C de l'Est

Av de les Drassanes

Drassanes

Rambla dels Caputxins

Plaça del Teatre

Rambla de Santa Mònica

C de l'Arc del Teatre

C d'Escudellers

Plaça d Portal de la Pa

0   200 m
0   0.1 miles

Sights

Palau Güell
PALACE

1 ◉ Map p50, D4

Finally reopened in its entirety in 2012 after several years of refurbishment, this is a magnificent example of the early days of Gaudí's fevered architectural imagination. The extraordinary neo-Gothic mansion, one of the few major buildings of that era raised in Ciutat Vella, gives an insight into its maker's prodigious genius. (☎93 472 57 75; www.palauguell.cat; Carrer Nou de la Rambla 3-5; adult/concession/under 10 €12/9/free; ☉10am-8pm Tue-Sun; Ⓜ Drassanes)

MACBA
ARTS CENTRE

2 ◉ Map p50, B2

Designed by Richard Meier and opened in 1995, MACBA has become the city's foremost contemporary art centre, with captivating exhibitions for the serious art lover. The permanent collection is on the ground floor and dedicates itself to Spanish and Catalan art from the second half of the 20th century, with works by Antoni Tàpies, Joan Brossa and Miquel Barceló, among others, though international artists, such as Paul Klee, Bruce Nauman and John Cage, are also represented. (Museu d'Art Contemporani de Barcelona; ☎93 481 33 68; www.macba.cat; Plaça dels Àngels 1; adult/concession/under 12 €10/8/free; ☉11am-7.30pm Mon & Wed-Fri, 10am-9pm Sat, 10am-3pm Sun & holidays; Ⓜ Universitat)

Local Life
Medieval Intrigue

Gaudí died at the 15th-century **Antic Hospital de la Santa Creu** (Former Hospital of the Holy Cross; Map p50, B3; ☎93 270 16 21; www.bcn.cat; Carrer de l'Hospital 56; ☉9am-8pm Mon-Fri, to 2pm Sat; Ⓜ Liceu), which now houses Catalonia's national library, an arts school and the Institute for Catalan Studies. Visit the grand readingrooms beneath broad Gothic stone arches, where you'll also find temporary exhibitions. Its delightful, if somewhat frayed, colonnaded courtyard has a popular cafe.

Centre de Cultura Contemporània de Barcelona
BUILDING

3 ◉ Map p50, B2

A complex of auditoriums, exhibition spaces and conference halls opened here in 1994 in what had been an 18th-century hospice, the Casa de la Caritat. The courtyard, with a vast glass wall on one side, is spectacular. With 4500 sq metres of exhibition space in four separate areas, the centre hosts a constantly changing program of exhibitions, film cycles and other events. (CCCB; ☎93 306 41 00; www.cccb.org; Carrer de Montalegre 5; adult/concession/under 12 for 1 exhibition €6/4/free, 2 exhibitions €8/6/free, Sun 3-8pm free; ☉11am-8pm Tue-Sun; Ⓜ Universitat)

Top Tip

Art Passport

Barcelona's best bargain for art lovers is the **Articket BCN** (www.articketbcn.org; €30), which gives you entry to six museums for a fraction of what you'd pay if you bought individual tickets. The museums are: MACBA; Centre de Cultura Contemporánia de Barcelona; Fundació Antoni Tàpies; Fundació Joan Miró; Museu Nacional d'Art de Catalunya; Museu Picasso.

Església de Sant Pau del Camp

CHURCH

4 Map p50, B5

The best example of Romanesque architecture in the city is the dainty little cloister of this church. Set in a somewhat dusty garden, the 12th-century church also boasts some Visigothic sculptural detail on the main entrance. (☎93 441 00 01; Carrer de Sant Pau 101; adult/concession €3/2; ⊗10am-1pm & 4-7pm Mon-Sat; Ⓜ Paral·lel)

Eating

El Colectivo

CAFE €

5 Map p50, B2

A relaxed little cafe on a quiet Raval street, El Colectivo makes excellent cake (carrot, pineapple, you name it), creative *bocadillos* (filled rolls) and good coffee. The shop-window seating is perfect for street watching, the decor is simple and minimal with a single row of wooden tables, and there's always good jazz playing in the background. Tapas are served on Thursdays and Fridays. (☎93 318 63 80; Carrer del Pintor Fortuny 22; bocadillos from €4; ⊗9am-9pm Mon-Wed, 9am-midnight Thu, 9am-2am Fri & Sat; 🤶; Ⓜ Catalunya)

Mam i Teca

CATALAN €€

6 Map p50, B3

A tiny place with half a dozen tables, Mam i Teca is as much a lifestyle choice as a restaurant. Locals drop in and hang at the bar, and diners are treated to Catalan dishes made with locally sourced products and that adhere to Slow Food principles (such as cod fried in olive oil with garlic and red pepper, or pork ribs with chickpeas). (☎93 441 33 35; Carrer de la Lluna 4; mains €9-12; ⊗1-4pm & 8pm-midnight Mon, Wed-Fri & Sun, 8pm-midnight Sat; Ⓜ Sant Antoni)

Flax & Kale

VEGETARIAN €€

7 Map p50, A2

A far cry from the vegie restaurants of old, Flax & Kale marks a new approach (for Barcelona, at least), that declares that going meat-free does not mean giving up on choice or creativity, and is entirely possible in stylish surroundings. There are gluten-free and vegan options, and dishes include tacos with guacamole, aubergine, shiitake mushrooms and sour cashew cream, or Penang red curry. (☎93 317 56 64; www.teresacarles.com; Carrer dels Tallers 74; mains €12.50-16.50; ⊗10am-11.30pm; 🤶; Ⓜ Universitat)

JUP3OLE/GETTY IMAGES ©

Pulled pork tacos

Caravelle

INTERNATIONAL €€

8 Map p50, B3

A bright little joint, beloved of the hipster element of El Raval and anyone with a discerning palate. Tacos as you've never tasted them (cod, lime *alioli* and radish, and pulled pork with roast corn and avocado); a superior steak sandwich on homemade brioche with pickled celeriac; and all manner of soul food. (☑93 317 98 92; www.caravelle.es; Carrer del Pintor Fortuny 31; mains €10-13; ☺9.30am-5.30pm Mon, 9.30am-1am Tue-Fri, 10am-1am Sat, 10am-5.30pm Sun; ⓂLiceu)

Suculent

CATALAN €€

9 Map p50, C4

Michelin-starred chef Carles Abellan adds to his stable with this old-style bistro, which showcases the best of Catalan cuisine. From the cod brandade to the oxtail stew with truffled sweet potato, only the best ingredients are used. Be warned that the prices can mount up a bit, but this is a great place to sample regional highlights. (☑93 443 65 79; www.suculent.com; Rambla del Raval 43; mains €13-21; ☺1-4pm & 8.30-11.30pm Wed-Sun; ⓂLiceu)

Dos Trece

INTERNATIONAL €€

10 Map p50, B3

Lively, sunny and fun, Dos Trece is great for brunches (including vegie and vegan options) that are available all day, as well as late-night bites. The menu ranges from juicy burgers to a more sophisticated rack of lamb, and the bar serves a good array of cocktails. There are a few tables outside, next to the kids' playground. (☑93 301 73 06; www.dostrece.es; Carrer del Carme 40; mains €10-15; ☺10am-midnight; �ⓂLiceu)

Drinking

La Confitería

BAR

11 Map p50, B5

This is a trip into the 19th century. Until the 1980s it was a confectioner's shop, and although the original cabinets are now lined with booze, the look of the place barely changed with its conversion into a laid-back bar. A quiet enough spot for a house *vermut* (€3; add your own soda) in the early evening. (Carrer de Sant Pau 128; ⏱7.30pm-2.30am Mon-Thu, 6pm-3.30am Fri, 5pm-3.30am Sat, 12.45pm-2.45am Sun; MParal·lel)

Casa Almirall   BAR

 12   Map p50, A3

In business since the 1860s, this unchanged corner bar is dark and intriguing, with Modernista decor and a mixed clientele. There are some great original pieces in here, such as the marble counter and the cast-iron statue of the muse of the Universal Exposition, held in Barcelona in 1888. (www.casaalmirall.com; Carrer de Joaquín Costa 33; ⏱6pm-2.30am Mon-Thu, 6.30pm-3am Fri, noon-3am Sat, noon-12.30am Sun; MUniversitat)

El Drapaire   BAR

13   Map p50, B2

Part of the recent explosion in the craft-beer scene, this cosy, beamed tavern has been given a new lease of life and now has 13 taps, featuring Spanish and international beers of all styles. There are tapas and platters of cheese and charcuterie to share. (☎607 466446; Carrer de les Sitges 11; ⏱5pm-1am Sun-Thu, to 2am Fri & Sat; MCatalunya)

Bar Pastís   BAR

14   Map p50, D4

A French cabaret theme (with lots of Piaf in the background) dominates this tiny, cluttered classic. It's been going, on and off, since the end of WWII.

Bar Pastís

You'll need to be in here before 9pm to have any hope of sitting, getting near the bar or anything much else. On some nights it features live acts, usually performing French *chansons*. (www.barpastis.com; Carrer de Santa Mònica 4; ⏱7.30pm-2am; MDrassanes)

Marmalade   BAR

 15   Map p50, B3

The golden hues of this backlit bar and restaurant beckon seductively through the glass facade. There are various distinct spaces, decorated in different but equally sumptuous styles, and a pool table next to the bar. Cocktails are big business here, and a selection of them are €5 all night.

STEFANO POLITI MARKOVINA/ALAMY STOCK PHOTO ©

(www.marmaladebarcelona.com; Carrer de la Riera Alta 4-6; ⏱6.30pm-2.30am Mon-Wed, 10am-2.30am Thu-Sun; Ⓜ Sant Antoni)

Moog   CLUB

16 Map p50, D4

This fun and minuscule club is a standing favourite with the downtown crowd. In the main dance area, DJs dish out house, techno and electro, while upstairs you can groove to a nice blend of indie and occasional classic-pop throwbacks. Admission is €5. (www.masimas.com/moog; Carrer de l'Arc del Teatre 3; ⏱midnight-5am Mon-Thu & Sun, to 6am Fri & Sat; Ⓜ Drassanes)

Entertainment

Gipsy Lou   LIVE MUSIC

17 Map p50, A3

A louche little bar that packs 'em in for live music from rumba to pop to flamenco, along with occasional storytelling events, and whatever else Felipe feels like putting on. There are decent bar snacks to keep you going on a long night of pisco sours, the house special. (www.gipsylou.com; Carrer de Ferlandina 55; ⏱8pm-2.30am Sun-Thu, 8pm-3am Fri & Sat; Ⓜ Sant Antoni)

Shopping

Fantastik   ARTS & CRAFTS

18 Map p50, A2

Over 400 products, including a Mexican skull rattle, robot moon explorer

Local Life
Avante-Garde Cinema
Less than a decade old, the beautifully designed **Filmoteca de Catalunya** (Map p50, C4; ☎93 567 10 70; www.filmoteca.cat; Plaça de Salvador Seguí 1-9; adult/concession €4/3; ⏱screenings 5-10pm, ticket office 10am-3pm & 4-9.30pm Tue-Sun; Ⓜ Liceu) has a two-screen cinema, as well as a library, bookshop, cafe and exhibition space. It shows unusual fare you won't find elsewhere, from obscure arthouse works through to directorial classics by European and American greats.

from China and recycled plastic zebras from South Africa, are to be found in this colourful shop, which sources its items from Mexico, India, Bulgaria, Russia, Senegal and 20 other countries. (☎93 301 30 68; www.fantastik.es; Carrer de Joaquín Costa 62; ⏱11am-2pm & 4-8.30pm Mon-Fri, noon-9pm Sat; Ⓜ Universitat)

Holala! Plaza   FASHION

19 Map p50, B2

Backing on to Carrer de Valldonzella, where it boasts an exhibition space (Gallery) for temporary art displays, this Ibiza import is inspired by that island's long established (and somewhat commercialised) hippie tradition. Vintage clothes are the name of the game, along with an eclectic program of exhibitions and activities. (www.holala-ibiza.com; Plaça de Castella 2; ⏱11am-9pm Mon-Sat; Ⓜ Universitat)

Explore

La Ribera &
Parc de la Ciutadella

In La Ribera is one of Barcelona's most beguiling corners: El Born. The old town's epicentre in medieval times, leafy Passeig del Born is again abuzz, crammed with bars, restaurants and boutiques. Adding to the neighbourhood's appeal, La Ribera also boasts the Museu Picasso, Barcelona's mightiest Gothic church, a wonderful market and the largest park in downtown Barcelona.

The Sights in a Day

☼ In a bid to avoid the crowds, get to the **Museu Picasso** (p58) early, then take a guided tour of the **Palau de la Música Catalana** (p68) to fully appreciate the genius and eccentricity of Modernisme. The **Mercat de Santa Caterina** (p68) is perfect for stocking up for a picnic lunch in the **Parc de la Ciutadella** (pictured left; p68).

☀ Explore the park after lunch, then settle into a pew to admire the grace and splendour of the **Basílica de Santa Maria del Mar** (p62). The church is just as beautiful on the outside, so make for our favourite vantage point, **La Vinya del Senyor** (p73), until evening falls.

☾ The dining options in El Born are limitless, but we'd start with tapas at convivial **Cal Pep** (p65), followed by creative global dishes at **El Atril** (p70). After dinner, enjoy a nightcap at laid-back **Rubí** (p73).

For a local's night out in El Born, see p64.

Top Sights

Museu Picasso (p58)

Basílica de Santa Maria del Mar (p62)

◯ Local Life

Tapas & Bar-Hopping in El Born (p64)

♥ Best of Barcelona

Tapas

Bormuth (p70)

El Xampanyet (p65)

Cal Pep (p65)

Euskal Etxea (p65)

Bar del Pla (p65)

Bars

Rubí (p73)

La Vinya del Senyor (p73)

Juanra Falces (p74)

Getting There

Ⓜ **Metro** Jaume I station (line 4), on the southwestern side of La Ribera, is close to everything.

Ⓜ **Metro** Urquinaona (lines 1 and 4) is handy for the Palau de la Música Catalana, while Arc de Triomf (line 1) is good for Parc de la Ciutadella.

Top Sights
Museu Picasso

Pablo Picasso spent many years in Barcelona and, suitably, the city hosts the world's foremost museum dedicated to the artist's formative years and his extraordinary early talent; the cubist paintings for which he is best known are largely absent, but this is nonetheless a world-class gallery that traces his development as an artist. The building – five contiguous medieval stone mansions that span five centuries and yet have seamlessly become one – is itself a perfectly conceived work of art.

◉ Map p66, D3

www.museupicasso.bcn.cat

Carrer de Montcada 15-23

adult/concession/child all collections €14/7.50/free, permanent collection €11/7/free, temporary exhibitions €4.50/3/free

🕑9am-7pm Tue, Wed & Fri-Sun, to 9.30pm Thu

Ⓜ Jaume I

Cloister, Museu Picasso

Don't Miss

The Child Artist

Rooms 1 & 2 The collection opens with sketches and oils from Picasso's earliest years in Málaga and La Coruña (around 1893–95), and leads on to his formative years in Barcelona. Some of his self-portraits and the portraits of his parents, which date from 1896, are evidence enough of his precocious talent. *Retrato de la Tía Pepa* (Portrait of Aunt Pepa), done in Málaga in 1896, shows the incredible maturity of his brushstrokes and his ability to portray character – at the tender age of 15.

Early Barcelona Days

Rooms 3 & 5 Picasso's early endeavours show a youthful talent searching for his style. In Room 3, his *Ciència i Caritat* (Science & Charity; painted in 1897 at age 16) is proof that, had he wanted, Picasso would have made a fine conventional artist. In Room 5, his studies of the styles of Velázquez and El Greco are fascinating insights into an artist perfecting his craft.

The Catalan Avant-Garde

Room 4 After a period spent in Horta de Sant Joan, he came back to Barcelona and joined what was known as the 'Catalan avant-garde'. The work *Poeta Decadente* (Decadent Poet) is a portrait of his new friend Jaume Sabartés, who would remain one of Picasso's lifelong confidants – and later be the all-but-official curator of Picasso's works.

☑ Top Tips

▶ Understand this gallery for what it is: a fascinating insight into Picasso's early work with scarcely a cubist masterpiece in sight.

▶ Buy tickets online to avoid the long queues.

▶ Entry is free after 3pm Sunday and on the first Sunday of the month.

▶ Consider buying the Articket BCN (see boxed text, p52) for combined admission to this and five other museums for €30.

✗ Take a Break

On Picasso's last visit to the city in 1934, El Xampanyet (p65) had already been open five years; it's still great for tapas.

Traditional Spanish tapas with subtle creative twists are the order of the day at young-at-heart Bar del Pla (p65), a little further northwest along Carrer de Montcada.

The Blue Period

Room 8 Before cubism took him across unexplored creative frontiers, Picasso went through his first thematic adventure – the Blue Period. Lasting from 1901 to 1904, it coincided with his last years spent living in Barcelona. His nocturnal blue tinted views of *Terrats de Barcelona* (Rooftops of Barcelona) are cold and cheerless, and yet somehow spectrally alive.

The Rose Period

Room 9 After the muted colours of the Blue Period, Picasso's palette fills with warm hues of pinks and oranges during his Rose Period, which unfolded in 1905. Harlequins, circus performers and acrobats make their appearance in his work. Although painted toward the end of this period, *Arlequí* (Harlequin) is characteristic of the vibrant paintings from this time.

Early Cubism

Room 11 Picasso's masterworks lie elsewhere, but by 1917 his style was hinting at the cubist forms to come. During a six-month stay in Barcelona in 1917, he painted *Passeig de Colom* and Blanquita Suárez, which bear strong evidence of what was to follow. Another fine work here is the *Glass and Tobacco Packet* still-life painting, a simple and beautiful work.

Museu Picasso

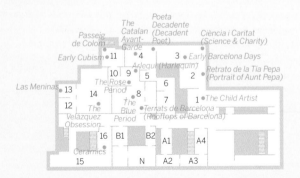

Understand
History of the Museum

Allegedly it was Picasso himself who proposed the museum's creation, to his friend and personal secretary, Jaume Sabartés, a Barcelona native, in 1960. Three years later, the 'Sabartés Collection' was opened, as a museum bearing Picasso's name would have been met with censorship – Picasso's opposition to the Franco regime was well known. The Museu Picasso we see today opened in 1983, and gradually expanded with donations from Salvador Dalí and Sebastià Junyer Vidal, among others, though most artworks were bequeathed by Picasso himself. His widow, Jacqueline Roque, also donated 41 ceramic pieces and the *Woman with Bonnet* painting after Picasso's death.

The Velázquez Obsession

Rooms 12–14 The extent to which Picasso was influenced by the great masters is evident in these rooms, which contain an extraordinary 58-painting study of Diego Velázquez' masterpiece *Las Meninas* (which hangs in the Museo del Prado in Madrid). Painted in Cannes in 1957, these will satisfy your longing for Picasso's signature cubist style.

Ceramics

Room 15 What is also special about the Museu Picasso is its showcasing of his work in lesser-known mediums. The last rooms contain engravings and some 40 ceramic pieces completed throughout the latter years of his unceasingly creative life. You'll see plates and bowls decorated with simple, single-line drawings of fish, owls and other animal shapes, typical for Picasso's daubing on clay.

Top Sights
Basílica de Santa Maria del Mar

Nothing prepares you for the singular beauty of the Basílica de Santa Maria del Mar. Barcelona's most stirring Gothic structure, the church stands serenely amid the crowds and clutter of buildings in El Born. In contrast to the tight warren of neighbouring streets, a real sense of light and space pervades the entire sanctuary of the church. Its interior is close to perfection wrought in stone, making this a worthy rival to La Catedral and La Sagrada Família for the affections of visitors to the city.

⊙ Map p66, D4

✆ 93 310 23 90

www.santamariadelmar barcelona.org

Plaça de Santa Maria del Mar

incl guided tour 1-5pm €8

⊙ 9am-8pm

Ⓜ Jaume I

Ceiling detail, Basílica de Santa Maria del Mar

Don't Miss

Main Sanctuary

The pleasing unity of form and symmetry of the church's central nave and two flanking aisles owed much to the rapidity with which the church was built in the 14th century – a mere 59 years, which must be a record for a major European house of worship. The slender, octagonal pillars create an enormous sense of lateral space bathed in the light of stained glass.

Ceiling & Side Chapels

Even before anarchists gutted the church in 1909 and again in 1936, Santa Maria always lacked superfluous decoration. Gone are the gilded chapels that weigh heavily over so many Spanish churches, while the splashes of colour high above the nave are subtle – unusually and beautifully so. It all serves to highlight the church's fine proportions, purity of line and sense of space.

The Porters

Look closely at the stones throughout the main sanctuary. One day a week during construction, the city's *bastaixos* (porters) carried these stones on their backs from the royal quarry in Montjuïc to the construction site. The memory of them lives on in reliefs in the main doors and stone carvings in the church, a reminder that this was conceived as a people's church.

El Fossar de les Moreres

Opposite the church's southern flank, an eternal flame burns high over a sunken square. This was El Fossar de les Moreres (the Mulberry Cemetery), where Catalan resistance fighters were buried after the siege of Barcelona ended in defeat in September 1714 during the War of the Spanish Succession.

☑ Top Tips

▶ Take a guided tour (offered 1pm to 5pm) to visit the roof terrace and crypt (€8).

▶ If your purpose is spiritual, try to be here for the daily mass at 7.30pm.

▶ Ask in the gift shop in case evening baroque music recitals are scheduled.

✕ Take a Break

Admire the western facade of the church while enjoying tapas and drinks at one of the outdoor tables of Bubó (p65).

Another fine spot for dining or drinking with a basilica view is at one of two balcony tables at La Vinya del Senyor (p73).

Local Life
Tapas & Bar-Hopping in El Born

If there's one place that distils Barcelona's enduring cool to its essence and provides a snapshot of all that's irresistible about this city, it has to be El Born, the tangle of streets surrounding the Basílica de Santa Maria del Mar. Its secret is simple: this is where locals go for an authentic Barcelona night out.

❶ Passeig del Born

Most nights, and indeed most things, in El Born begin along Passeig del Born, one of the prettiest little boulevards in Europe. It's a place to sit as much as to promenade. It's a graceful setting beneath the trees from which El Born's essential appeal is obvious – thronging people, brilliant bars and architecture that springs from a medieval film set.

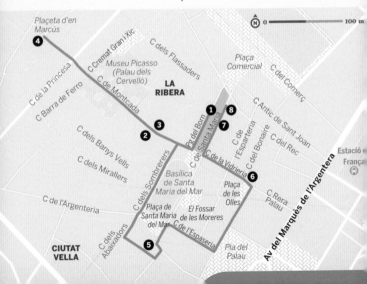

❷ Catalan Tapas

Push through the crowd to order a *cava* (sparkling wine) and an assortment of tapas at **El Xampanyet** (☏ 93 319 70 03; Carrer de Montcada 22; ⏲ noon-4pm & 7-11pm Tue-Sat, noon-4pm Sun; Ⓜ Jaume I), one of the city's best-known *cava* bars, in business since 1929. Star dishes include tangy *boquerones en vinagre* (white anchovies in vinegar) and there's high-quality seafood served from a can in the Catalan way.

❸ Basque Delicacies

Having taken your first lesson in Barcelona-style tapas it's time to compare it with the *pintxos* (Basque tapas of food morsels perched atop pieces of bread) lined up along the bar at **Euskal Etxea** (☏ 93 310 21 85; Placeta de Montcada 1; tapas €1.95; ⏲ 10am-12.30am Sun-Thu, to 1am Fri & Sat; Ⓜ Jaume I), a real slice of San Sebastián.

❹ Spain with a Twist

This detour to the northern limits of El Born is worth the walk. At first glance, the tapas at informal **Bar del Pla** (☏ 93 268 30 03; www.bardelpla.cat; Carrer de Montcada 2; mains €12-16; ⏲ noon-11pm Mon-Thu, to midnight Fri & Sat; Ⓜ Jaume I) are traditionally Spanish, but the riffs on a theme display an assured touch. Try the ham and roasted-meat croquettes or the marinated salmon, yoghurt and mustard.

❺ Tapas with a View

Back in the heart of El Born, in the shadow of the Basílica de Santa Maria del Mar, pastry chef Carles Mampel operates **Bubó** (☏ 93 268 72 24; www.bubo.es; Carrer de les Caputxes 6 & 10; tapas from €5; ⏲ 10am-9pm Mon-Thu & Sun, to 11pm Fri & Sat; Ⓜ Barceloneta). If you're not already sated, try the salted cod croquettes at one of the outdoor tables inching onto the lovely square.

❻ An Enduring Star

Boisterous **Cal Pep** (☏ 93 310 79 61; www.calpep.com; Plaça de les Olles 8; mains €13-20; ⏲ 7.30-11.30pm Mon, 1-3.45pm & 7.30-11.30pm Tue-Sat, closed last 3 weeks Aug; Ⓜ Barceloneta) is one of Barcelona's lasting stars. It can be difficult to snaffle a bar stool from which to order gourmet bar snacks such as *cloïsses amb pernil* (clams with ham); so if it's full, order a drink and wait. It's always worth it.

❼ El Born's Favourite Bar

El Born Bar (☏ 93 319 53 33; Passeig del Born 26; ⏲ 10am-2am Mon-Sat, noon-1.30am Sun; 🛜; Ⓜ Jaume I) effortlessly attracts everyone from cool thirty-somethings from all over town to locals who pass judgement on Passeig del Born's passing parade. Its staying power depends on a good selection of beers, spirits, and *empanadas* and other snacks.

❽ The Last Mojito

So many Barcelona nights end with a mojito, and El Born's biggest and best are to be found at **Cactus Bar** (☏ 93 310 63 54; www.cactusbar.cat; Passeig del Born 30; ⏲ 3pm-3am; Ⓜ Jaume I). The outdoor tables next to Passeig del Born are the perfect way to wind down the night.

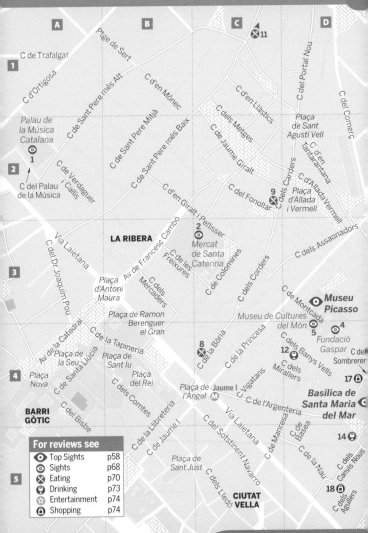

A

B

C

D

C de Trafalgar

Ptge de Sert

C d'en Mònec

C de Sant Pere més Alt

C d'Ortigosa

Palau de la Música Catalana
1

C de Sant Pere més Mitjà

C de Verdaguer i Callís

C del Palau de la Música

C de Sant Pere més Baix

C d'en Giralt i Pellisser

C d'en Llàstics

C dels Metges

C de Jaume Giralt

C del Fonollar

9

C del Portal Nou

Plaça de Sant Agustí Vell

C d'en Tantarantana

C del Comerç

C dels Carders

C d'Allada Vermell

Plaça d'Allada i Vermell

LA RIBERA

Av de Francesc Cambó

C de les Freixures

Via Laietana

C del Dr Joaquim Pou

Plaça d'Antoni Maura

C dels Mercaders

2

Mercat de Santa Caterina

C de Colomines

C dels Corders

C dels Assaonadors

C de Montcada

Museu Picasso

Plaça de Ramon Berenguer el Gran

C de la Tapineria

Plaça de la Seu Llúcia

Plaça de Sant Iu

8

C de la Bòria

Museu de Cultures del Món
5

C de la Princesa

4

Fundació Gaspar

C dels Banys Vells

12

C dels Mirallers

C del Sombrerer

17

Plaça Nova

Av de la Catedral

C de Santa Llúcia

C dels Comtes

Plaça del Rei

Plaça de l'Àngel

Jaume I

C de Vigatans

C de l'Argentería

Basílica de Santa Maria del Mar

BARRI GÒTIC

C del Bisbe

C de la Llibreteria

C de la Jaume I

Via Laietana

C de Manresa

C de Basea

14

C del Sotstinent Navarro

Plaça de Sant Just

C dels Lledó

CIUTAT VELLA

C de la Nau

C dels Canvis Nous

18

C dels Aguilers

E

P

Pg de Lluís Companys

Pg de Pujades

F

G

N

0   200 m
0   0.1 miles

H

1

Pg de Picasso

C de la Princesa

C de la Fusina

C de la Ribera

C Comercial

Born Centre de Cultura i Memòria

2

Zoo de Barcelona

3

⊗ 7

5

⊗ 3

Plaça Comercial

C dels ...assaders

19

10

16

13

C del Comerç

C Antic de Sant Joan

Pg del Born

C de l'Esparteria

C del Rec

C de Montcada

C Rera Palau

6

Estació de França

Av del Marquès de l'Argentera

Pg de Circumval·lació

4

C de Santa Maria

Pla del Palau

LA RIBERA

Pg d'Isabel II

C de la Marquesa

C d'Ocata

Barceloneta

M

C del Doctor Aiguader

Ronda del Litoral

LA BARCELONETA

5

Sights

Palau de la Música Catalana
ARCHITECTURE

1 Map p66, A2

This concert hall is a high point of Barcelona's Modernista architecture, a symphony in tile, brick, sculpted stone and stained glass. Built by Domènech i Montaner between 1905 and 1908 for the Orfeo Català musical society, it was conceived as a temple for the Catalan Renaixença (Renaissance). (📞93 295 72 00; www.palaumusica.cat; Carrer de Palau de la Música 4-6; adult/concession/child €18/11/free; ⏰guided tours 10am-3.30pm, to 6pm Easter, Jul & Aug; Ⓜ Urquinaona)

Mercat de Santa Caterina
MARKET

2 Map p66, C3

Come shopping for your tomatoes at this extraordinary-looking produce market, designed by Enric Miralles and Benedetta Tagliabue to replace its 19th-century predecessor. Finished in 2005, it is distinguished by its kaleidoscopic and undulating roof, held up above the bustling produce stands, restaurants, cafes and bars by twisting slender branches of what look like grey steel trees. (📞93 319 57 40; www.mercatsantacaterina.com; Avinguda de Francesc Cambó 16; ⏰7.30am-3.30pm Mon, Wed, Sat, to 8.30pm Tue, Thu, Fri, closed afternoons Jul & Aug; Ⓜ Jaume I)

Local Life
A Walk in the Park

The handsomely landscaped **Parc de la Ciutadella** (Map p66, G2; Passeig de Picasso; 🚻; Ⓜ Arc de Triomf) is a local favourite for a leisurely promenade. The park is the site of Catalonia's regional parliament, the city zoo, some eye-catching buildings and the monumental **Cascada** (waterfall) created between 1875 and 1881 by Josep Fontsère with the help of a young Antoni Gaudí.

Born Centre de Cultura i Memòria
HISTORIC BUILDING

3 Map p66, E3

Launched to great fanfare in 2013, as part of the events held for the tercentenary of the Catalan defeat in the War of the Spanish Succession, this cultural space is housed in the former Mercat del Born, a handsome 19th-century structure of slatted iron and brick. Excavation in 2001 unearthed remains of whole streets flattened to make way for the much-hated citadel (*ciutadella*) – these are now on show on the exposed subterranean level. (📞93 256 68 51; http://elbornculturaimemoria.barcelona.cat; Plaça Comercial 12; centre free, exhibition spaces adult/concession/child €6/4.20/free; ⏰10am-8pm Tue-Sun Mar-Sep, 10am-7pm Tue-Sat, to 8pm Sun Oct-Feb; Ⓜ Barceloneta)

Fundació Gaspar

GALLERY

4 ◎ Map p66, D4

Set in a stunning Gothic palazzo next to the Museu Picasso, the Fundació Gaspar opened in November 2015 with the intention of complementing the works of other galleries and museums around town by bringing contemporary artists who have yet to exhibit here or whose work explores new concepts and styles. The exhibitions are on the 1st floor, while the ground floor is taken up with a graceful courtyard, where you'll find the Café Gaspar and a shop specialising in edgy, arty gifts. (☎ 93 887 42 48; www.fundaciogaspar.org; Carrer de Montcada 25; adult/concession/ under 12 €5/3/free; ⊙10am-8pm Tue, Wed, Fri-Sun, to 9.30pm Thu; Ⓜ Jaume I)

Museu de Cultures del Món

MUSEUM

5 ◎ Map p66, D4

The Palau Nadal and the Palau Marquès de Lló, which once housed the Museu Barbier-Mueller and the Museu Tèxtil respectively, reopened in 2015 to the public as the site of a new museum, the Museum of World Cultures. Exhibits from private and public collections, including many from the Museu Etnològic (p130) on Montjuïc, take the visitor on a trip through the ancient cultures of Africa, Asia, the Americas

CISCO PELAY/ALAMY STOCK PHOTO ©

Museu de Cultures del Món

and Oceania. There's a combined ticket with the Museu Egipci and Museu Etnològic for €12. (☎93 256 23 00; http://museuculturesmon.bcn.cat; Carrer de Montcada 12; adult/concession/child €5/3.50/ free, temporary exhibition €2.20/1.50/free, 3-8pm Sun & 1st Sun of month free; ☷10am-7pm Tue-Sat, to 8pm Sun; Ⓜ Jaume I)

Eating

Paradiso
SMOKERY €

 6 Map p66, E4

A kind of Narnia-in-reverse, Paradiso is fronted with a snowy-white space, not much bigger than a wardrobe, and in itself reason enough to linger, with pastrami sandwiches, smoked duck and other home-cured delights from the Rooftop Smokehouse team, best known for its food trucks. (☎639 310671; www. rooftopsmokehouse.com; Carrer de Rera Palau

---

Local Life
Fish for People in the Know

There's no sign, but locals know where to head for a seafood feast. At **Passadís del Pep** (Map p66, E5; ☎93 310 10 21; www.passadis.com; Pla del Palau 2; mains €19-24; ☷1.15-3.45pm & 8.30-11.30pm Mon-Sat; Ⓜ Barceloneta) the raw materials are delivered daily from fishing ports along the Catalan coast. There's no menu – what's on offer depends on what the sea has surrendered that day. Just head down the long, ill-lit corridor and entrust yourself to its care.

4; mains €8; ☷cocktail bar 7pm-2am Sun-Thu, to 3am Fri & Sat, pastrami bar noon-2am Sun-Thu, to 3am Fri & Sat; Ⓜ Barceloneta)

Bormuth
TAPAS €

 7 Map p66, E3

Opened on the pedestrian Carrer del Rec in 2013, Bormuth has tapped into the vogue for old-school tapas with modern-times service and decor, and serves all the old favourites – *patatas bravas* (potato chunks in a slightly spicy tomato sauce), *ensaladilla* (Russian salad), tortilla – along with some less predictable and superbly prepared numbers (try the chargrilled red pepper with black pudding). (☎93 310 21 86; Carrer del Rec 31; tapas from €4; ☷1pm-midnight; 🛜; Ⓜ Jaume I)

Cat Bar
VEGAN €

8 Map p66, C4

This tiny little joint squeezes in a vegan kitchen, a great selection of local artisanal beers and a smattering of live music. The food mostly centres on a list of different burgers, plus a gluten-free dish of the day, plus tapas and hummus. The beers change regularly, but there is always one wheat, one porter, one gluten-free and an IPA. (Carrer de la Bòria 17; mains €6.50-8.50; ☷6-11.30pm Mon-Wed, 1-11pm Thu-Sat; 🛜🗲; Ⓜ Jaume I)

El Atril
INTERNATIONAL €€

9 Map p66, C2

Aussie owner Brenden is influenced by culinary flavours from all over the globe, so while you'll see plenty of

Patatas bravas

tapas (the *patatas bravas* are recommended for their homemade sauce), you'll also find kangaroo fillet, salmon and date rolls with mascarpone, chargrilled turkey with fried yucca, and plenty more. (☏ 93 310 12 20; www.atril barcelona.com; Carrer dels Carders 23; mains €11-15; ⏱ noon-midnight Mon-Thu, to 1am Fri & Sat, 11.30am-11.30pm Sun; 🛜; Ⓜ Jaume I)

between a leek and an onion; February and March only) or salt-strewn *padron* peppers, move on to grilled sardines speckled with parsley, then tackle the meaty monkfish roasted in white wine and garlic. (☏ 93 319 50 88; www.tallerdetapas.com; Passeig del Born 36; mains €10-15; ⏱ 8am-midnight Sun-Thu, to 1am Fri & Sat; 🛜; Ⓜ Barceloneta)

Casa Delfín   CATALAN €€

🔟 ✖️ Map p66, E3

One of Barcelona's culinary delights, Casa Delfín is everything you dream of when you think of Catalan (and Mediterranean) cooking. Start with the tangy and sweet *calçots* (a cross

Nakashita   JAPANESE €€

11 ✖️ Map p66, C1

Brazil's particular immigration story means it has a tradition of superb Japanese food, and the Brazilian chef at Nakashita is no slouch, turning out excellent sashimi, maki rolls, soft shell

Understand

Catalan Gothic Architecture

Historical Context

The emergence of the soaring Gothic style of architecture in France in the 13th century coincided with an expanding Catalan empire, the rise of a trading class and a burgeoning mercantile sphere of influence. The enormous cost of building the grand new monuments could thus be covered by the steady increase in Barcelona's wealth.

The architectural style reflected developing building techniques. The introduction of flying buttresses and ribbed vaulting in ceilings allowed engineers to raise edifices loftier and seemingly lighter than ever before. The pointed arch became standard and great rose windows offered a way to bring light inside these enormous spaces.

Catalan Difference

Catalan Gothic rarely followed the same course as the style in northern Europe. Decorations are more sparing; another distinctive characteristic is the triumph of breadth over height. While northern European cathedrals reach for the sky, Catalan Gothic structures push to the sides, stretching the vaulting design to the limit.

The Saló del Tinell in the Museu d'Història de Barcelona (p34), with a parade of 15m arches (among the largest ever built without reinforcement) holding up the roof, is a perfect example of Catalan Gothic. Another is the present home of the Museu Marítim (p82), Barcelona's medieval shipyards. In churches too, the Catalans opted for robust shape and lateral space – step into the Basílica de Santa Maria del Mar (p62) and you'll soon get the idea.

Also a notable departure from northern Gothic styles is the lack of spires and pinnacles. Bell towers tend to terminate in a flat or nearly flat roof. Occasional exceptions prove the rule. The main facade of Barcelona's Catedral, with its three gnarled and knobbly spires, does vaguely resemble the outline that confronts you in the cathedrals of Chartres or Cologne. But then this was a 19th-century addition, admittedly constructed to an existing medieval design.

Most of Barcelona's Gothic heritage lies within the boundaries of the old city but a few examples can be found beyond, notably the Museu-Monestir de Pedralbes (p139) in Sarrià.

crab and kakiage (a mix of tempura). One of the best Japanese restaurants in the city, with just a handful of tables – book if you can. (☏ 93 295 53 78; www.nakashitabcn.com; Carrer del Rec Comtal 15; mains €15-20; ⏱ 1.30-4.30pm & 8.30pm-midnight; 🛜; Ⓜ Arc de Triomf)

Drinking

Rubí
BAR

12 🍸 Map p66, D4

With its boudoir lighting and cheap mojitos, Rubí is where the Born's cognoscenti head for a nightcap – or several. It's a narrow, cosy space – push through to the back where you might just get one of the coveted tables, with superior bar food, from Vietnamese rolls to more traditional selections of cheese and ham. (☏ 647 773707; Carrer dels Banys Vells 6; ⏱ 7.30pm-2.30am Sun-Thu, to 3am Fri & Sat; Ⓜ Jaume I)

Guzzo
COCKTAIL BAR

13 🍸 Map p66, E3

A swish but relaxed cocktail bar, run by much-loved Barcelona DJ Fred Guzzo, who is often to be found at the decks, spinning his delicious selection of funk, soul and rare groove. You'll also find frequent live-music acts of consistently decent quality, and a funky atmosphere at almost any time of day. (☏ 93 667 00 36; www.guzzo.es; Plaça Comercial 10; ⏱ 6pm-3am Tue-Thu, to 3.30am Fri & Sat, noon-3am Sun; 🛜; Ⓜ Barceloneta)

Wine and olive tasting

La Vinya del Senyor
WINE BAR

14 🍸 Map p66, D5

Relax on the *terrassa*, which lies in the shadow of the Basílica de Santa Maria del Mar, or crowd inside at the tiny bar. The wine list is as long as *War and Peace* and there's a table upstairs for those who opt to sample by the bottle rather than the glass. (☏ 93 310 33 79; www.lavinyadelsenyor.com; Plaça de Santa Maria del Mar 5; ⏱ noon-1am Mon-Thu, noon-2am Fri & Sat, noon-midnight Sun; 🛜; Ⓜ Jaume I)

Local Life
A Blissful Spa

With low lighting and relaxing perfumes wafting around you, **Aire de Barcelona** (Map p66, E2; ☎93 295 57 43; www.airedebarcelona.com; Passeig de Picasso 22; thermal baths & aromatherapy Mon-Thu €31, Fri-Sun €33; ☺10am-10pm Mon-Thu & Sun, 10am-2am Fri & Sat; Ⓜ Arc de Triomf) could be the perfect way to end a day. Hot, warm and cold baths, steam baths and options for various massages, including on a slab of hot marble, make for a delicious hour or so. Book ahead and bring a swimming costume.

Juanra Falces   COCKTAIL BAR

15 🍷 Map p66, E3

Transport yourself to a Humphrey Bogart movie in this narrow little bar, formerly (and still, at least among the locals) known as Gimlet. White-jacketed bar staff with all the appropriate aplomb will whip you up a gimlet or any other classic cocktail (around €10) that your heart desires. (☎93 310 10 27; Carrer del Rec 24; ☺8pm-3am Tue-Sat, 10pm-3am Sun & Mon; Ⓜ Jaume I)

Entertainment
Palau de la Música Catalana   CLASSICAL MUSIC

A feast for the eyes, this Modernista confection is also the city's most traditional venue for classical and choral music (see 1 ◎ Map p66, A2), although it has a wide-ranging program, including flamenco, pop and – particularly – jazz. Just being here for a performance is an experience. In the foyer, its tiled pillars all a-glitter, sip a pre-concert tipple. (☎93 295 72 00; www.palaumusica.cat; Carrer de Palau de la Música 4-6; from €15; ☺box office 9.30am-9pm Mon-Sat, 10am-3pm Sun; Ⓜ Urquinaona)

Shopping
Hofmann Pastisseria   FOOD

16 🔒 Map p66, E4

With its painted wooden cabinets, this bite-sized gourmet patisserie, linked to the prestigious Hofmann cooking school, has an air of timelessness. Choose between jars of delicious chocolates, the renowned croissants (in various flavours) and more dangerous pastries, or an array of cakes and other sweet treats. (☎93 268 82 21; www.hofmann-bcn.com; Carrer dels Flassaders 44; ☺9am-2pm & 3.30-8pm Mon-Thu, to 8.30pm Fri & Sat, 9am-2.30pm Sun; Ⓜ Barceloneta)

Casa Gispert   FOOD

17 🔒 Map p66, D4

The wonderful, atmospheric and wood-fronted Casa Gispert has been toasting nuts and selling all manner of dried fruit since 1851. Pots and jars piled high on the shelves contain an unending variety of crunchy tidbits: some roasted, some honeyed, all of them moreish. Your order is shouted over to the till, along with the price, in a display of old-world accounting.

Loisaida

(☎93 319 75 35; www.casagispert.com; Carrer dels Sombrerers 23; ⊘10am-2pm & 4-8pm Mon-Sat; Ⓜ Jaume I)

Vila Viniteca

WINE

18 Map p66, D5

One of the best wine stores in Barcelona (and there are a few...), this place has been searching out the best local and imported wines since 1932. On a couple of November evenings it organises what has become an almost riotous wine-tasting event in Carrer dels Agullers and surrounding lanes, at which cellars from around Spain present their young new wines. (☎902

327777; www.vilaviniteca.es; Carrer dels Agullers 7; ⊘8.30am-8.30pm Mon-Sat; Ⓜ Jaume I)

Loisaida

CLOTHING, ANTIQUES

19 🔒 Map p66, E3

A sight in its own right, housed in what was once the coach house and stables for the Royal Mint, Loisaida (from the Spanglish for 'Lower East Side') is a deceptively large emporium of colourful, retro and somewhat preppy clothing for men and women, costume jewellery, music from the 1940s and '50s and some covetable antiques. (☎93 295 54 92; www.loisaidabcn. com; Carrer dels Flassaders 42; ⊘11am-9pm Mon-Sat, 11am-2pm & 4-8pm Sun; Ⓜ Jaume I)

Explore

Barceloneta & the Beaches

Barcelona's waterfront is a fascinating corner of the city – a place where avant-garde public art is juxtaposed with the gritty thorough-fares of Barceloneta, an 18th-century fisherfolk's district. It's in the restaurants of the latter that you'll find the city's best seafood and rice dishes, while beaches stretch away to the north.

The Sights in a Day

Begin with a journey through Catalan history at the **Museu d'Història de Catalunya** (p82), take a return trip aboard the **Teleférico del Puerto** (p82) for fine waterfront views, then head for **L'Aquàrium** (p82), one of Spain's best aquariums.

Most afternoons in Barceloneta revolve around food and beaches. For the former, we suggest a feast of small plates of seafood at **Kaiku** (p84) or **La Cova Fumada** (p79). The perfect response to such gastronomic excess is to lie down, and this is best done at any beach that takes your fancy from Barceloneta to Port Olímpic and beyond.

There are loads of great settings for a drink in the area. Festive **Can Paixano** (p78) has ever-flowing glasses of *cava* (sparkling wine), while **Absenta** (p86) and **Ké?** (p87) draw a more bohemian crowd. For Mediterranean views, opt for one of the summertime **chiringuitos** (p86), where you can sip cocktails while digging your heels in the sand. Near Port Olímpic is another row of waterfront bars, which adopt more of a nightclub vibe as the evening progresses.

For a local's day by the beach, see p78.

Local Life

Barceloneta Sea & Seafood (p78)

Best of Barcelona

Seafood Restaurants

Barraca (p86)

La Cova Fumada (p79)

Bars

Absenta (p86)

Can Paixano (p78)

Vaso de Oro (p79)

Chiringuitos (p86)

Getting There

M Metro Drassanes (line 3) is best for the southwestern end of the port, Barceloneta (line 4) for Barceloneta, and Ciutadella Vila Olímpica (line 4) for the beaches and Port Olímpic.

Bus Numbers 17, 39 and 64 all converge on Barceloneta.

Cable Car If you're coming from Montjuïc, the Teleférico del Puerto is best.

Local Life
Barceloneta Sea & Seafood

Barcelona's Mediterranean roots are nowhere more pronounced than in Barceloneta, a seaside peninsula with a salty air and an enduring relationship with the sea. As often as not, this is one area where locals outnumber tourists, at least on weekends when the city's restaurants and beaches throng with a predominantly local crowd.

❶ The Cava Crowd

Welcome to Barcelona as it once was. It doesn't come any more authentic than **Can Paixano** (☎93 310 08 39; Carrer de la Reina Cristina 7; ◷9am-10.30pm Mon-Sat; Ⓜ Barceloneta), one of the best old-style *cava* (sparkling wine) bars in Barcelona. This ageless bar serves up the pink stuff in elegant little glasses, provided you can elbow your way through the crowds to order.

❷ Seaside Views

Head up to the top floor of the **Museu d'Història de Catalunya** (you don't need to buy a ticket) to the elegant seafood restaurant **1881** (📞93 221 00 50; www.sagardi.com; Plaça de Pau Vila 3; mains €18-30; ⏰1pm-1am Sun-Thu, to 3am Fri & Sat; 🛜; Ⓜ Barceloneta). Step out onto the terrace for a lovely view over the marina.

❸ Beer & Prawns

If you like buzzing, overflowing bars, high-speed staff ready with a smile, a cornucopia of tapas and the illusion, in here at least, that Barcelona hasn't changed in decades, come to **Vaso de Oro** (📞933 19 30 98; www.vasodeoro.com; Carrer de Balboa 6; tapas €4-12; ⏰noon-midnight; Ⓜ Barceloneta). This place has ice-cold draught beer and the tapas are delicious (try the grilled prawns).

❹ A Waterfront Stroll

Maybe it's a good thing the metro doesn't reach the beach at Barceloneta, obliging you to walk down the sunny portside promenade of **Passeig de Joan de Borbó**. Megayachts sway gently on your right as you bowl down a street crackling with activity.

❺ Mouth-Watering Tapas

There's no sign and the setting is decidedly downmarket, but tiny **La Cova Fumada** (📞93 221 40 61; Carrer del Baluard 56; tapas €4-8; ⏰9am-3.20pm Mon-Wed, 9am-3.20pm & 6-8.15pm Thu & Fri, 9am-1pm Sat; Ⓜ Barceloneta) always packs in a crowd. The secret? Mouth-watering small plates cooked to perfection in the small open kitchen.

❻ Market Buzz

Set in a modern glass and steel building in the heart of the neighbourhood, the **Mercat de la Barceloneta** (📞93 221 64 71; www.mercatdelabarceloneta.com; Plaça de la Font 1; ⏰7am-3pm Mon-Thu & Sat, 7am-8pm Fri; Ⓜ Barceloneta) has the usual array of fresh veg and seafood stalls, as well as the good sit-down restaurant El Guindilla. Across the street, don't miss **Baluard Barceloneta**, one of the city's best bakeries.

❼ Iconic Drinking Den

Bar Leo (Carrer de Sant Carles 34; ⏰noon-9.30pm; Ⓜ Barceloneta) is a hole-in-the-wall drinking spot plastered with images of late Andalucian singer and heart-throb Bambino, with a jukebox mostly dedicated to flamenco. For a youthful, almost entirely *barcelonin* crowd, Bar Leo is it!

❽ Barcelona's Beaches

There are prettier beaches elsewhere on earth, but none so handy for the world's coolest city. **Platja de Sant Sebastià**, closest to Barceloneta, yields to **Platja de la Barceloneta**, and both are broad and agreeably long sweeps of sand.

❾ An Olympic Port

A 1.25km promenade shadows the waterfront all the way to the restaurant-lined marina of **Port Olímpic**. An eye-catcher on the approach from Barceloneta is Frank Gehry's giant copper *Peix* (Fish) sculpture, while just to the north is the enticing **Platja de Nova Icària**.

Via Laietana

C de Sant Pere més Baix

C del Portal Nou

Plaça d'Antoni Maura

LA RIBERA

C del Comerç

C Comercial

Pg de Picasso

Parc de la Ciutadella

Zoo de Barcelona

C de la Princesa

C del Rec

C de la Bòria

C de la Ribera

Pg de Circumval·lació

Plaça de la Seu

Plaça Nova

BARRI GÒTIC

Jaume I

Pg del Born

Av del Marquès de l'Argentera

Estació de França

Plaça de Sant Just

Plaça de Santa Maria del Mar

Pla del Palau

C d'Ocata

LA RIBERA

Barceloneta

C del Doctor Aiguader

Ronda del Litoral

C de la Mediterrània

Plaça de Sant Miquel

CIUTAT VELLA

Via Laietana

Pg d'Isabel II

C de la Reina Cristina

C del Doctor Aiguader

C de Balboa

C de Ginebra

C de Pau Vila

Plaça de la Maquinista

C de Ferran

C d'Avinyó

C d'En Gignàs

15

14

2

Museu d'Història de Catalunya

8

11

Plaça de la Font

C dels Escudellers

C Ample

C de la Mercè

Pg de Colom

Mirador del Port Vell

Pg de la Barceloneta

16

C del Mar

Plaça del Duc de Medinaceli

Ronda del Litoral

Marina

Moll de la Barceloneta

C del Almirall Aixada

Rambla de Santa Mònica

Port de Barcelona

Pg d'Itaca

Plaça de l'Ictineo

L'Aquàrium

Moll del Rellotge

C del Judi

Drassanes

C de Josep Anselm Clavé

Moll de la Fusta

3

C del Mar

Moll de Balears

PORT VELL

Plaça del Portal de la Pau

17

Moll d'Espanya

C de l'Escar

1

Museu Marítim

Moll de les Drassanes

Pg de Joan de Borbó

10

Plaça del Mar

Port Vell

4

Teleférico del Puerto

E — Universitat Pompeu Fabra
Parc de Carles I
C de Wellington
M — Ciutadella Vila Olímpica
C de Moscou
C de Salvador Espriu
Plaça dels Voluntaris
Av del Litoral
F
Moll de Mestral
G
Moll de Gregal
H
C de Ramon Trias Fargas
C de la Marina
Port Olímpic
1

g de Circumval·lació
C de Trelawny
Av del Litoral
Ronda del Litoral
2

Pg de Salvat Papasseit
Pg Marítim de la Barceloneta
Platja de la Barceloneta
Parc de la Barceloneta
3

C d'Andrea Dòria
LA BARCELONETA
C de Guitert
6
13
12
C de Sant Carles
Platja de Sant Sebastià
de l'Almirall Cervera
4

5
7
Molokai UP enter
Mediterranean Sea

latja de ant Miquel

N
0 — 400 m
0 — 0.2 miles

For reviews see	
◉ Sights	p82
✗ Eating	p83
⊖ Drinking	p86
⌂ Shopping	p87

5

Sights

Museu Marítim
MUSEUM

1 Map p80, A5

These mighty Gothic shipyards shelter the Museu Marítim, a remarkable relic from Barcelona's days as the seat of a seafaring empire. Highlights include a full-sized replica (made in the 1970s) of Don Juan of Austria's 16th-century flagship, fishing vessels, antique navigation charts and dioramas of the Barcelona waterfront. (☏93 342 99 20; www.mmb.cat; Avinguda de les Drassanes; adult/child €7/3.50, 3-8pm Sun free; ◷10am-8pm; ⧟Drassanes)

Museu d'Història de Catalunya
MUSEUM

2 Map p80, C3

Inside the Palau de Mar, this worthwhile museum takes you from the Stone Age through to the early 1980s. It is a busy hotchpotch of dioramas, artefacts, videos, models, documents and interactive bits: all up, an entertaining exploration of 2000 years of Catalan history. Signage is in Catalan/Spanish. (Museum of Catalonian History; ☏93 225 47 00; www.mhcat.net; Plaça de Pau Vila 3; adult/child €4.50/3.50, last Tue of the month Oct-Jun free; ◷10am-7pm Tue & Thu-Sat, to 8pm Wed, to 2.30pm Sun; ⧟Barceloneta)

L'Aquàrium
AQUARIUM

3 Map p80, C4

It is hard not to shudder at the sight of a shark gliding above you, displaying its toothy, wide-mouthed grin. But

Top Tip

Seaside Spin

Stretching over 4km from Barceloneta to Parc del Fòrum, the beachside bike path makes a breezy setting for a spin. Open-air cafes and restaurants are ideal pit stops along the way. Loads of places hire bikes, including **BarcelonaBiking** (Map p80, A3; ☏656 356300; www.barcelonabiking.com; Baixada de Sant Miquel 6; bike hire per hr/24hr €5/15, tour €21; ◷10am-8pm, tour 11am; ⧟Jaume I, Liceu) in the Barri Gòtic and **My Beautiful Parking** (Map p80, B2; ☏93 186 73 65; www.mybeautifulparking.com; Carrer de la Bòria 17; bike hire per hr/24hr €5/14; ◷10am-3pm & 4.30-8pm; ⧟Jaume I) in La Ribera.

the 80m shark tunnel is the highlight here. One of Europe's largest marine exhibits, L'Aquàrium has the world's best Mediterranean collection and plenty of colourful fish from as far off as the Red Sea, the Caribbean and the Great Barrier Reef. All up, some 11,000 fish (including a dozen sharks) of 450 species reside here. (☏93 221 74 74; www.aquariumbcn.com; Moll d'Espanya; adult/child €20/15, dive €300; ◷9.30am-11pm Jul & Aug, to 9pm Sep-Jun; ⧟Drassanes)

Teleférico del Puerto
CABLE CAR

4 Map p80, D5

This cable car strung across the harbour to Montjuïc provides an eagle-eye view of the city. The cabins float between the Torre de Sant Sebastià (Barceloneta) and Miramar (Montjuïc), with a midway stop at the Torre de Jaume I in front of the World Trade Center. At the top of the Torre de Sant Sebastià is a restaurant, Torre d'Alta Mar. (www.telefericodebarcelona.com; Passeig Escullera; one way/return €11/16.50; ⏱11am-7pm Mar-Oct, to 5.30pm Nov-Feb; 🚌17, 39, 64, Ⓜ Barceloneta)

Molokai SUP Center WATER SPORTS

5 ◎ Map p80, E4

This respected outfit will give you a crash course in stand-up paddle-boarding. In addition to the two-hour beginner's class, Molokai can help you improve your technique (in interme-diate and advanced lessons – all in two-hour blocks); gear and wetsuit is included. Or if you'd rather just hire a SUP board, they can get you out on the sea in no time. (📞93 221 48 68; www.molokaisupcenter.com; Carrer de Meer 39; 2hr lesson €55, SUP rental per hour €15; Ⓜ Barceloneta)

Eating

Filferro TAPAS €

6 🍴 Map p80, E3

One of the few spots in Barceloneta where the focus isn't on seafood, Filferro has a loyal following for its good-value tapas, *bocadillos* (filled rolls), salads and pastas. It has a warmly lit

ALIONABRIUKOVA/SHUTTERSTOCK ©

Museu Marítim

Local Life

Beachfront Art

American Rebecca Horn's striking sculptural tribute to Barceloneta, *Homenatge a la Barceloneta* is an eye-catching column of rusted-iron-and-glass cubes on Platja de Sant Sebastià. Erected in 1992, it pays homage to the beach bars and restaurants that disappeared around the time of the Olympic Games, and hence it has earned the respect of even the crustiest old-timers in the neighbourhood.

and eclectically furnished interior, or you can dine at an outdoor table on the square (popular with families, with a playground just a few steps away). (☑93 221 98 36; Carrer de Sant Carles 29; tapas €5-7, mains €8-13; ⊙10am-1am Tue-Sun; 🛜🖉; Ⓜ Barceloneta)

Guingueta de la Barceloneta

SPANISH €

7 Map p80, E4

Part of Carles Abellan's gastronomic empire, this open-sided beachside spot serves up snacks, sandwiches and salads, though cocktails (around €11) are the big draw (as is the sea view). (Platja de Sant Sebastià; sandwiches €6-12; ⊙9am-midnight Mar-Nov; Ⓜ Barceloneta)

Jai-Ca

SEAFOOD €

8 Map p80, D3

Jai-Ca is a much-loved eatery that serves up juicy grilled prawns, flavour-rich anchovies, tender octopus, deca-dent razor clams and other seafood favourites to ever-growing crowds as the evening progresses. The *turbio* (Galician white wine), sangria and cold draughts are ideal refreshments after a day on the beach. (☑93 268 32 65; Carrer de Ginebra 13; tapas €4-8; ⊙9am-11.30pm Mon-Sat; Ⓜ Barceloneta)

El Ben Plantat

INTERNATIONAL €

9 Map p80, E3

A welcome addition to seafood-centric Barceloneta, El Ben Plantat serves a varied menu of small plates, with excellent vegetarian choices (hummus, guacamole and chips, tofu pâté, stuffed marinated mushrooms). On weekdays you'll also find multicourse lunch specials (mussels with potatoes, homemade falafel, sausage with ratatouille, vegetable croquettes) – good value at €9. (☑93 624 38 32; Carrer de Sant Carles 21; tapas €5-10; ⊙1-4pm & 8.30-11.30pm Wed-Mon; 🖉; Ⓜ Barceloneta)

Kaiku

SEAFOOD €€

10 Map p80, D5

Overlooking the waterfront at the south end of Barceloneta, Kaiku has a solid reputation for creative seafood plates. Mouth-watering ingredients are sourced from the nearby fish market, and artfully prepared in dishes like crayfish with mint, swordfish carpaccio with avocado and sundried tomatoes, chilli-smeared tuna with green apples and mushrooms, and the outstanding rice dishes for two. (☑93 221 90 82; www.restaurantkaiku.cat; Plaça del Mar 1; mains for 2 €28-36; ⊙1-3.30pm Tue-Sun; Ⓜ Barceloneta)

Understand

The Changing Fortunes of Catalonia

Catalan identity is a multifaceted phenomenon, but Catalans are, more than anything else, united by the collective triumphs and shared grievances of the region's tumultuous past.

The Catalan golden age began in the early 12th century when Ramon Berenguer III, who already controlled Catalonia and parts of southern France, launched the region's first seagoing fleet. In 1137 his successor, Ramon Berenguer IV, was betrothed to the one-year-old heiress to the Aragonese throne, thereby giving Catalonia sufficient power to expand its empire out into the Mediterranean. By the end of the 13th century, Catalan rule extended to the Balearic Islands and Catalonia's seaborne trade brought fabulous riches.

But storm clouds were gathering; weakened by a decline in trade and foreign battles, Catalonia was vulnerable. And when Fernando became king of Aragón in 1479 and married Isabel, Queen of Castile, Catalonia became a province of Castile. Catalonia resented its new subordinate status but could do little to overturn it. After backing the losing side in the War of the Spanish Succession (1702–13), Barcelona rose up against the Spanish crown whose armies besieged the city from March 1713 until 11 September 1714. The victorious Felipe V abolished Catalan self-rule, built a huge fort (the Ciutadella) to watch over the city, banned writing and teaching in the Catalan language, and farmed out Catalonia's colonies to other European powers.

Trade again flourished from Barcelona in the following centuries, and by the late 19th and early 20th centuries there were growing calls for greater self-governance to go with the city's burgeoning economic power. However, after Spanish general Francisco Franco's victory in 1939, Catalan Francoists and the dictator's army shot in purges at least 35,000 people, most of whom were either anti-Franco or presumed to be so. Over time, the use of Catalan in public was banned, all street and town names were changed into Spanish, and Castellano Spanish was the only permitted language in schools and the media. Franco's lieutenants remained in control of the city until his death in 1975 and the sense of grievance in Barcelona remains – though today it's directed against the central government in Madrid. Pride in Catalan culture has never been greater, with talk of independence dominating the airwaves throughout Barcelona and the rest of Catalonia.

Can Maño
SPANISH €€

11 Map p80, D3

It may look like a dive, but you'll need to be prepared to wait before being squeezed in at a packed table for a raucous night of *raciones* (full-plate-size tapas servings; posted on a board at the back) over a bottle of *turbio* – a cloudy white plonk. The seafood is abundant with first-rate squid, shrimp and fish served at rock-bottom prices. (Carrer del Baluard 12; mains €8-14; ⊘9am-4pm Tue-Sat & 8-11pm Mon-Fri; Ⓜ Barceloneta)

Barraca
SEAFOOD €€€

12 Map p80, E4

This buzzing space has a great location fronting the Mediterranean – a key reference point in the excellent seafood dishes served here. Start off with a cauldron of chilli-infused clams, cockles and mussels before moving

on to the lavish paellas and other rice dishes, which steal the show. (📞93 224 12 53; www.barraca-barcelona.com; Passeig Marítim de la Barceloneta 1; mains €19-24; ⊘12.30pm-midnight; Ⓜ Barceloneta)

Drinking

Absenta
BAR

13 Map p80, E3

Decorated with old paintings, vintage lamps and curious sculpture (including a dangling butterfly woman and face-painted TVs), this whimsical and creative drinking den takes its liquor seriously. Stop in for the house-made vermouth or for more bite try one of the many absinthes on hand. Just go easy: with an alcohol content of 50% to 90%, these spirits have kick! (www.absentabar.es; Carrer de Sant Carles 36; ⊘7pm-1am Tue & Wed, from 11am Thu-Mon; Ⓜ Barceloneta)

BlackLab
MICROBREWERY

14 Map p80, C3

Inside the historic Palau de Mar, BlackLab was Barcelona's first brewhouse to open way back in 2014. With 20 taps (including 18 house-made brews, including saisons, double IPAs and dry stouts), it's an impressive operation, and the brewmasters are constantly experimenting with new flavours. (📞93 221 83 60; www.blacklab.es; Plaça Pau Vila 1; ⊘noon-1.30am; Ⓜ Barceloneta)

Local Life

Waterfront Markets

On weekends, art, craft and antique lovers shouldn't miss these appealing markets. At the base of La Rambla, the small **Port Antic Market** (Map p80, A5; Plaça del Portal de la Pau; ⏰10am-8pm Sat & Sun; MDrassanes) has old photographs, frames, oil paintings, records, cameras, vintage toys and other odds and ends. At the **Feria de Artesanía del Palau de Mar** (Moll del Dipòsit; ⏰11am-8.30pm Sat & Sun; MBarceloneta) near the Palau de Mar, artisans sell a range of crafty items, including jewellery, clothing and crafty souvenirs. Take the pedestrian-only Rambla de Mar to reach the **Mercado de Pintores** (Map p80, C4; Passeig d'Ítaca; ⏰10am-8pm Sat & Sun; MDrassanes), where local artists sell their paintings.

The Mint   COCKTAIL BAR

15 Map p80, C3

Named after the prized cocktail ingredients, this mojito-loving drinkery has a little something for everyone. Linger upstairs with the grown-ups to peruse the first-rate house-infused gins (over 20 on hand, including creative blends like lemongrass and Jamaican pepper), or head downstairs with the kids to the brick-vaulted cellars, where red lights and driving beats create a more celebratory vibe. (☎647 737707; Passeig d'Isabel II, 4; ⏰7.30pm-2.30am; MBarceloneta)

Ké?   BAR

16 Map p80, D3

An eclectic and happy crowd hangs about this small bohemian bar run by a friendly Dutchman. Pull up a padded 'keg chair' or grab a seat on one of the worn lounges at the back and join in the animated conversation wafting out over the street. Outdoor seating in summer, just a few steps from Barceloneta's market. (Carrer del Baluard 54; ⏰noon-2am; MBarceloneta)

Shopping

Maremàgnum   MALL

17 Map p80, C5

Created out of largely abandoned docks, this buzzing shopping centre, with its bars, restaurants and cinemas, is pleasant enough for a stroll virtually in the middle of the old harbour. The usual labels are on hand, including the youthful Spanish chain Mango, mega-retailer H&M and eye-catching fashions from Barcelona-based Desigual. Football fans will be drawn to the paraphernalia at FC Botiga. (☎93 225 81 00; www.maremagnum.es; Moll d'Espanya 5; ⏰10am-10pm; MDrassanes)

Explore

Passeig de Gràcia & L'Eixample

L'Eixample, bisected by the monumental Passeig de Gràcia, is the sophisticated alter ego to Barcelona's old city. This is where Modernisme left its most enduring mark and it's here that some of the city's most iconic architectural landmarks reside. With elegant shops, terrific restaurants and pulsating nightlife, it all adds up to one of the city's most rewarding neighbourhoods.

The Sights in a Day

 The earlier you get to **Casa Batlló** (p92) and **La Pedrera** (p90) the better your chances of avoiding the worst crowds. If you linger over the weird-and-wonderful detail of these sites, you could easily spend a couple of hours in each, which should just leave time to admire **Casa Amatller** (p98) and get the low-down on contemporary art at the **Fundació Antoni Tàpies** (p99).

Take a break from museums with a tapas feast at Carles Abellan's inventive **Tapas 24** (p101), followed by some window-shopping along elegant Passeig de Gràcia. Finish off the afternoon at the **Museu del Modernisme Barcelona** (p100).

L'Eixample nights can be long and liquid, but we suggest one last Modernista fling: dinner at **Casa Calvet** (p104), with its otherwise inaccessible Gaudí interiors. **Les Gens Que J'Aime** (p105) is a great place to ease into the evening, while **Dry Martini** (p105) is another favourite. End the night with a touch of live salsa at **Antilla BCN** (p105).

For a local's day of shopping in L'Eixample, see p94.

 Top Sights

La Pedrera (p90)

Casa Batlló (p92)

Local Life

Shopping in the Quadrat d'Or (p94)

Best of Barcelona

Tapas
Tapas 24 (p101)

Cata 1.81 (p102)

Bars
Dry Martini (p105)

Les Gens Que J'Aime (p105)

Monvínic (p95)

Getting There

Ⓜ **Metro** Passeig de Gràcia (lines 2, 3 and 4) and Diagonal (lines 3, 5 and 7) are in the heart of L'Eixample.

Ⓜ **Metro** Around L'Eixample's perimeter are Catalunya, Universitat, Hospital Clínic, Verdaguer and Girona.

🚇 **FGC** Provença and Passeig de Gràcia stations.

Top Sights
La Pedrera

One of Passeig de Gràcia's, and indeed Barcelona's, most beautiful Modernista structures, La Pedrera – officially called Casa Milà after its owners, but nicknamed La Pedrera (the Stone Quarry) by bemused locals who watched Gaudí build it from 1905 to 1910 – is in the top tier of Gaudí's achievements. Conceived as an apartment block, its approach to space and to light and its blurring of the dividing line between decoration and functionality will leave you gasping at the sheer originality of it all.

Map p96, D2

www.lapedrera.com

Passeig de Gràcia 92

adult/concession/under 13/ under 7 €20.50/16.50/10.25/ free

9am-8.30pm Mar-Oct, to 6.30pm Nov-Feb

M Diagonal

Rooftop terrace, La Pedrera

Don't Miss

The Facade

The natural world was one of the most enduring influences on Gaudí's work, and La Pedrera's undulating grey stone facade evokes a cliff-face sculpted by waves and wind. The wave effect is emphasised by elaborate wrought-iron balconies that bring to mind seaweed washed up on the shore. The lasting impression is of a building on the verge of motion.

The Roof Terrace

Gaudí's blend of mischievous form with ingenious functionality is evident on the roof, with its clusters of chimneys, stairwells and ventilation towers that rise and fall atop the structure's wave-like contours like giant medieval knights. Some are unadorned, others are decorated with *trencadís* (ceramic fragments) and even broken *cava* bottles. The deep patios, which Gaudí treated like interior facades, flood the apartments with natural light.

Espai Gaudí

With 270 gracious parabolic arches, the Espai Gaudí feels like the fossilised ribcage of some giant prehistoric beast. At one point, 12 arches come together to form a palm tree. Watch out also for the strange optical effect of the mirror and hanging sculpture on the east side.

La Pedrera Apartment

Below the attic, the apartment (El Pis de la Pedrera) spreads out. Bathed in evenly distributed light, twisting and turning with the building's rippling distribution, the labyrinthine apartment is Gaudí's vision of domestic bliss. In the ultimate nod to flexible living, the apartment has no load-bearing walls: the interior walls could thus be moved to suit the inhabitants' needs.

☑ Top Tips

▶ La Pedrera is extremely popular: buy tickets online and arrive at opening time to avoid the worst of the crowds.

▶ Guided evening tours show the mysterious side of La Pedrera and end with a glass of *cava*. Reserve a spot in advance.

▶ On Fridays and Saturdays, from mid-June to early September, La Pedrera hosts open-air concerts on the roof.

✕ Take a Break

One block west of La Pedrera, **La Bodegueta Provença** (Map p96, C2; ☎ 93 215 17 25; www.labo degueta.cat; Carrer de Provença 233; mains €9-19, tapas €6-14; ⏱ 7am-1am Mon-Fri, 9am-1am Sat, 1pm-midnight Sun; 🛜; Ⓜ Diagonal) is a classy spot serving first-rate tapas and wines by the glass.

An excellent anytime choice (coffee and croissants, or tapas for lunch or dinner), Cerveseria Catalana (p101) lies two blocks south near the Rambla de Catalunya.

Top Sights
Casa Batlló

If La Sagrada Família is Gaudí's master symphony, Casa Batlló is his whimsical waltz – not to mention one of the weirdest-looking concoctions to emerge from his fantastical imagination. From the playful genius of its facade to its revolutionary experiments in light and architectural form (straight lines are few and far between), Casa Batlló, which was built as an anything-but-humble apartment block, is one of the most beautiful buildings in this city where competition for such a title is fierce.

⊙ Map p96, E3

www.casabatllo.es

Passeig de Gràcia 43

adult/concession/under 7
€22.50/19.50/free

⊙9am-9pm, last admission 8pm

Ⓜ Passeig de Gràcia

Facade of Casa Batlló

Don't Miss

The Facade

To Salvador Dalí it resembled 'twilight clouds in water'. Others see a more-than-passing resemblance to the impressionist masterpiece *Water Lilies* by Claude Monet. A Rorschach blot for our imagination, Casa Batlló's facade is exquisite and fantastical, sprinkled with fragments of blue, mauve and green tiles, and studded with wave-shaped window frames and mask-like balconies.

Sala Principal

The staircase wafts you to the 1st floor, where everything swirls in the main salon: the ceiling twists into a whirlpool-like vortex around its sun-like lamp; the doors, window and skylights are dreamy waves of wood and coloured glass in mollusc-like shapes. The sense of light and space here is extraordinary thanks to the wall-length window onto Passeig de Gràcia.

Back Terrace

Opening onto an expansive L'Eixample patio, Casa Batlló's back terrace is like a fantasy garden in miniature. It's a place where flowerpots take on strange forms and where the accumulation of *trencadís* (broken ceramic pieces) – a mere 330 of them on the building's rear facade – has the effect of immersing you in a kaleidoscope.

The Roof

Casa Batlló's roof, with the twisting chimney pots so characteristic of Gaudí's structures, is the building's grand crescendo. The eastern end represents Sant Jordi (St George) and the Dragon; one local name for Casa Batlló is the *casa del drac* (house of the dragon). The ceaseless curves of coloured tiles have the effect of making the building seem like a living being.

☑ Top Tips

▶ Queues to get in are frequent, so buy tickets online and go early in the morning.

▶ Although Casa Batlló stays open until 9pm, the last entry tickets are sold at 8pm.

▶ Even if you've already visited, return after sunset to see the facade illuminated in all its glory.

✗ Take a Break

Two short blocks down the hill and just off the other side of Passeig de Gràcia, Tapas 24 (p101) is one of Barcelona's most innovative tapas bars.

A short walk southwest of Casa Batlló, Monvínic (p95) has one of the best wine selections in the city, plus delicious sharing plates to accompany the fine quaffs.

Local Life
Shopping in the Quadrat d'Or

While visitors to L'Eixample do the sights, locals go shopping in the Quadrat d'Or (Golden Square), the grid of streets either side of Passeig de Gràcia. This is Barcelona at its most fashion- and design-conscious, which also describes a large proportion of L'Eixample's residents. All the big names are here, alongside boutiques of local designers who capture the essence of Barcelona cool.

1 The New Wave
You could spend an entire day along Passeig de Gràcia but detour for a moment to **Lurdes Bergada** (☏93 218 48 51; www.lurdesbergada. es; Rambla de Catalunya 112; ☉10.30am-8.30pm Mon-Sat; Ⓜ Diagonal), a boutique run by mother-and-son designer team Lurdes Bergada and Syngman Cucala. The classy men's and women's fashions use natural fibres and have attracted a cult following.

❷ The Sweet Life

Time for a break. And few pastry shops have such a long-established pedigree as **Mauri** (☎93 215 10 20; www.pastelerias mauri.com; Rambla de Catalunya 102; pastries from €3.50; ⏱8am-midnight Mon-Sat, 9am-4pm Sun; Ⓜ Diagonal). The plush interior is capped by an ornate fresco dating back to Mauri's first days in 1929. Its croissants and feather-light *ensaïmadas* (sweet buns) are near perfect.

❸ Modernista Jewellery

This is more than just any old jewellery store. The boys from **Bagués-Masriera** (☎93 216 01 74; www.bagues-masriera.com; Passeig de Gràcia 41; ⏱10am-8.30pm Mon-Fri, 11am-8pm Sat; Ⓜ Passeig de Gràcia) have been chipping away at precious stones and moulding metal since the 19th century, and many of the classic pieces here have a flighty, Modernista influence. Bagués backs it up with service that can be haughty, but owes much to old-school courtesies.

❹ Luxury Luggage

While bags and suitcases in every conceivable colour of buttersoft leather are the mainstay at **Loewe** (☎93 216 04 00; www.loewe.com; Passeig de Gràcia 35; ⏱10am-8.30pm Mon-Sat; Ⓜ Passeig de Gràcia), there is also a range of clothing for men and women, along with some stunning – and stunningly priced – accessories. The shop itself is worth a visit, housed in the **Casa Lleó Morera** (p98), and with some interior details by Domènech i Montaner.

❺ Say It With Chocolate

A sleek and modern temple to the brown stuff, **Cacao Sampaka** (☎93 272 08 33; www.cacaosampaka.com; Carrer del Consell de Cent 292; ⏱9am-9pm Mon-Sat; Ⓜ Passeig de Gràcia) doubles as a shop and cafe and is the perfect place to stock up with gifts to take back home. Select from every conceivable flavour (rosemary, anyone, or curry?), either in bar form or as individual choccies to fill your own elegant little gift box.

❻ Fine Wines

For superior souvenirs in liquid form, head to the state-of-the-art **Monvínic** (☎93 272 61 87; www.monvinic.com; Carrer de la Diputació 249; ⏱1-11pm Tue-Fri, 7-11pm Mon & Sat; Ⓜ Passeig de Gràcia), a veritable palace of wine with more than 3000 wines in its cellar, including some extremely rare finds. Try before you buy in the wine bar, and ask them to make you up a gift box for someone special back home.

❼ Chill Down

Cosmo (www.galeriacosmo.com; Carrer d'Enric Granados 3; ⏱10am-10pm Sun-Wed, to 11pm Thu, to midnight Fri & Sat; Ⓜ Universitat) is a bright, white cavernous space, dotted with colour from the exhibitions that adorn its high walls. It has a nice selection of teas, cakes and snacks. Set on a pleasant pedestrian strip, it's perfect for an evening tipple outside or in.

A B C D

1

C d'Alfons XII
Travessera de Gràcia
C d'Aribau
C de Tuset
C de Moià

Via Augusta

Plaça de Narcís Oller

C de Sèneca

C de Bonavista

C de Còrsega

Plaça de Joan Carles I

Palau del Baró Quadras
Diagonal M ⊙ 5
Fundació ⊙ 9
Suñol

⊙ 15
C de Pau Claris

La Pedrer

Av Diagonal

C de Balmes

C d'Enric Granados

C del Rosselló

Diagonal M Pg de Gràcia

2

C de Londres
C de Casanova
C de Paris

22 ⊙

C de Còrsega

C d'Aribau

Provença M

L'ESQUERRA DE L'EIXAMPLE

C de Mallorca

Rambla de Catalunya

13 ⊗

29 ⊗
4

Fundac
Antoni Tàpi

3

C de Villarroel

Plaça del Doctor Ferrer Cajigal

C de Muntaner

C de Provença

Plaça del Doctor Letamendi

C d'Aragó

Museu del Modernisme Barcelona

17
18 ⊗
⊗

20 ⊗

C d'Enric Granados

M Hospital Clínic

19 ⊗

C de Casanova

23 ⊙

Universitat Barcelon

4

C del Rosselló
C del Comte d'Urgell

C de València

C de Villarroel
C de Casanova

C de la Diputació

Plaça de Universit

Av de Roma
C d'Aragó

24 ⊗

C del Comte Borrell

C del Consell de Cent

Gran Via de les Corts Catalanes

C de Sepúlveda

Ronda

5

10 ⊗

11 Urgell M

For reviews see	
⊙ Top Sights	p90
⊙ Sights	p98
⊗ Eating	p101
⊙ Drinking	p105
⊙ Shopping	p106

E Verdaguer M **Av Diagonal** F G H
6
C de Sicília
C de Nàpols
C de Roger de Flor
C de Napòls

L'EIXAMPLE 1

Gran Via de les Corts Catalanes

❌ 14

31 C de Mallorca C de Girona C de Ballén Pg de Sant Joan

P 6 ◎
Palau C de València C d'Aragó
Montaner C de Roger de Llúria C del Bruc Plaça
33 de Tetuan

26 C del Consell de Cent M Girona M Tetuan 2

Passeig de C de la Diputació Pg de Sant Joan
Gràcia
C de Pau Claris
C de Casp

Casa Batlló C de Casp
Casa Amatller C d'Ausiàs Marc C d'Alí Bei
30 ◎ 3
1 C d'Ausiàs Marc Arc de
32 12 Triomf M 3
Casa Pg de Gràcia
Lleó ❌
Morera 21 Ronda de Sant Pere C de Trafalgar
Plaça Plaça de
de Joan Sant Pere
Carles I Plaça
7 Jardins d'Urquinaona
Sala de la Reina M Urquinaona C de Sant Pere més Alt
Fundació Victòria C d'Ortigosa
MAPFRE Urquinaona C de Sant Pere més Baix
27 M
25 28 Via Laietana 4
Catalunya LA
Plaça de RIBERA
Catalunya
M C de Bergara C Comtal
Universitat Plaça
C de Pelai d'Antoni
Catalunya Maura
C dels Tallers Plaça Plaça de
Nova la Seu
Plaça de La Rambla
Vicenç **BARRI**
C de Valldonzella Martorell **GÒTIC** Jaume I M
Plaça **EL RAVAL** 500 m 5
de Joan 0
Coromines 0 0.25 miles

Sights

Casa Lleó Morera
ARCHITECTURE

 1 Map p96, E3

Domènech i Montaner's 1905 contribution to the Manzana de la Discordia, with Modernista carving outside and a bright, tiled lobby in which floral motifs predominate, is perhaps the least odd-looking of the three main buildings on the block. Since 2014 part of the building has been open to the public (by guided tour only – a one-hour tour in English at 11am, and 'express tours' every 30 minutes), so you can appreciate the 1st floor, giddy with swirling sculptures, rich mosaics and whimsical decor. (📞93 676 27 33; www.casalleomorera.com; Passeig de Gràcia 35; guided tour adult/concession/under 12 €15/13.50/free, express tour adult/under 12 €12/free; ⏰10am-1.30pm & 3-7pm Tue-Sun; Ⓜ Passeig de Gràcia)

Recinte Modernista de Sant Pau
ARCHITECTURE

 2 Map p96, B1

Domènech i Montaner outdid himself as architect and philanthropist with the Modernista Hospital de la Santa Creu i de Sant Pau, redubbed in 2014 the 'Recinte Modernista'. It was long considered one of the city's most important hospitals, and only recently repurposed, its various spaces becoming cultural centres, offices and something of a monument. The complex, including 16 pavilions – together with the Palau de la Música Catalana (p68), a joint World

Heritage site – is lavishly decorated and each pavilion is unique. (📞93 553 78 01; www.santpaubarcelona.org; Carrer de Sant Antoni Maria Claret 167; adult/concession/under 16 €10/7/free; ⏰10am-6.30pm Mon-Sat, to 2.30pm Sun; Ⓜ Sant Pau/Dos de Maig)

Casa Amatller
ARCHITECTURE

 3 Map p96, E3

One of Puig i Cadafalch's most striking bits of Modernista fantasy, Casa Amatller combines Gothic window frames with a stepped gable borrowed from Dutch urban architecture. But the busts and reliefs of dragons, knights and other characters dripping off the main facade are pure caprice. The pillared foyer and staircase lit by stained glass are like the inside of some romantic castle. The building was renovated in 1900 for the chocolate baron and philanthropist Antoni Amatller (1851–1910). (📞93 461 74 60; www.amatller.org; Passeig de Gràcia 41; adult/child 6-12/under 6 1hr tour €15/7.50/free, 30min tour €12/7/free; ⏰11am-6pm; Ⓜ Passeig de Gràcia)

Fundació Antoni Tàpies

GALLERY

4 ⊙ Map p96, D3

The Fundació Antoni Tàpies is both a pioneering Modernista building (completed in 1885) and the major collection of leading 20th-century Catalan artist Antoni Tàpies. A man known for his esoteric work, Tàpies died in February 2012, aged 88; he left behind a powerful range of paintings and a foundation intended to promote contemporary artists. (☎93 487 03 15; www.fundaciotapies.org; Carrer d'Aragó 255; adult/concession €7/5.60; ☺10am-7pm Tue-Sun; Ⓜ Passeig de Gràcia)

Palau del Baró Quadras

ARCHITECTURE

5 ⊙ Map p96, D1

Puig i Cadafalch designed Palau del Baró Quadras (built 1902–06) in an exuberant Gothic-inspired style. The main facade is its most intriguing, with a soaring, glassed-in gallery. Take a closer look at the gargoyles and reliefs – the pair of toothy fish and the sword-wielding knight clearly have the same artistic signature as the architect behind Casa Amatller. Decor inside is eclectic, but dominated by Middle Eastern and East Asian themes. (☎93 467 80 00; www.llull.cat; Avinguda Diagonal 373; admission free; ☺8am-8pm Mon-Fri; Ⓜ Diagonal)

Casa Lleó Morera

Carrer d'Enric Granados

Half the city's population would like to live on Carrer d'Enric Granados. The pedestrianised end, at Carrer de la Diputació, is marked off by the Universitat de Barcelona gardens. The banter of diners can be heard at nearby restaurants as you wander rows of elegant apartments to the Plaça del Doctor Letamendi. From here, one lane of traffic trickles along up to Avinguda Diagonal (this end is also pedestrian only).

Palau Montaner   ARCHITECTURE

6 ⊙ Map p96, E2

Interesting on the outside and made all the more enticing by its gardens, this creation by Domènech i Montaner is spectacular on the inside. Completed in 1896, its central feature is a grand staircase beneath a broad, ornamental skylight. The interior is laden with sculptures (some by Eusebi Arnau), mosaics and fine woodwork. It is currently only open by guided tour, organised by the Fundació Tàpies and in Catalan only. (☏93 317 76 52; www.fundaciotapies.org; Carrer de Mallorca 278; adult/child €7/free; ☺guided tours 11am Sat; Ⓜ Passeig de Gràcia)

Sala Fundación MAPFRE   GALLERY

7 ⊙ Map p96, E4

Formerly the Fundación Francisco Godia, this stunning, carefully restored Modernista residence was taken over in late 2015 by the charitable cultural arm of Spanish insurance giants MAPFRE as a space for art and photography exhibitions. Housed in the Casa Garriga i Nogués, it is a stunning, carefully restored Modernista residence originally built for a rich banking family by Enric Sagnier in 1902–05. (☏93 401 26 03; www.fundacion mapfre.org; Carrer de la Diputació 250; adult/student/under 6 €6/3/free; ☺2-8pm Mon, 10am-8pm Tue-Sat, 11am-7pm Sun; Ⓜ Passeig de Gràcia)

Museu del Modernisme Barcelona   MUSEUM

8 ⊙ Map p96, D4

Housed in a Modernista building, the ground floor seems like a big Modernista furniture showroom. Several items by Antoni Gaudí, including chairs from Casa Batlló and a mirror from Casa Calvet, are supplemented by a host of items by his lesser-known contemporaries, including some typically whimsical, mock medieval pieces by Puig i Cadafalch. (☏93 272 28 96; www.mmbcn.cat; Carrer de Balmes 48; adult/concession/child 6-16/under 6 €10/7/5/free; ☺10.30am-7pm Tue-Sat, to 2pm Sun; Ⓜ Passeig de Gràcia)

Fundació Suñol   GALLERY

9 ⊙ Map p96, D2

Rotating exhibitions of portions of this private collection of mostly 20th-century art (some 1200 works in total) offer anything from Man Ray's photography to sculptures by Alberto

Giacometti. Over two floors, you are most likely to run into Spanish artists, anyone from Picasso to Jaume Plensa, along with a sprinkling of international artists. (☎93 496 10 32; www.fundaciosunol.org; Passeig de Gràcia 98; adult/concession €4/3; ⏱11am-2pm & 4-8pm Mon-Fri, 4-8pm Sat; Ⓜ Diagonal)

Eating

Copasetic
CAFE €

🔟 ❌ Map p96, C5

A fun and friendly cafe, decked out with retro furniture. The menu holds plenty for everyone, whether your thing is eggs Benedict, wild-berry tartlets or a juicy fat burger. There are lots of vegetarian, gluten-free and organic options, and superb (and reasonably priced) brunches on weekends. Wednesday night is ladies' night, with cheap cocktails. Lunch *menús* (Tuesday to Friday) cost between €9.50 and €11. (☎93 532 76 66; www.copasetic barcelona.com; Carrer de la Diputació 55; mains €8-12; ⏱10.30am-midnight Tue & Wed, 10.30am-1am Thu, 10.30am-2am Fri & Sat, 10.30am-5.30pm Sun; 🛜🍴; Ⓜ Rocafort)

Amaltea
VEGETARIAN €

⓫ ❌ Map p96, C5

The ceiling fresco of blue sky sets the scene in this popular vegetarian eatery. The *menús del día* (€8.70 and €10.70) offer dishes that change frequently with the seasons. At night, the set dinners (€11.50 and €15.50) offer good

value, and the homemade desserts are tempting. The place is something of an alternative lifestyle centre, with yoga, t'ai chi and belly-dancing classes. (☎93 454 86 13; www.restauranteamaltea.com; Carrer de la Diputació 164; mains €5-9; ⏱1-4pm & 8-11.30pm Mon-Sat; 🛜🍴; Ⓜ Urgell)

Tapas 24
TAPAS €€

⓬ ❌ Map p96, E3

Carles Abellan, master of the now-defunct Comerç 24 in La Ribera, runs this basement tapas haven known for its gourmet versions of old faves. Specials include the *bikini* (toasted ham and cheese sandwich – here the ham is cured and the truffle makes all the difference) and a thick black *arròs negre de sípia* (squid-ink black rice). (☎93 488 09 77; www.carlesabellan. com; Carrer de la Diputació 269; tapas €4-9; ⏱9am-midnight; 🛜; Ⓜ Passeig de Gràcia)

Cerveseria Catalana
TAPAS €€

⓭ ❌ Map p96, D3

The 'Catalan Brewery' is good for breakfast, lunch and dinner. Come for your morning coffee and croissant, or enjoy the abundance of tapas and *montaditos* (tapas on a slice of bread) at lunch. You can sit at the bar, on the pavement terrace or in the restaurant at the back. The variety of hot tapas, salads and other snacks draws a well-dressed crowd of locals and outsiders. (☎93 216 03 68; Carrer de Mallorca 236; tapas €4-11; ⏱8am-1.30am Mon-Fri, 9am-1.30am Sat & Sun; Ⓜ Passeig de Gràcia)

Local Life
Secret Dining Spot

True to name, **Speakeasy** (Map p96, B2; ☏93 217 50 80; www.speakeasy-bcn. com; Carrer d'Aribau 162-166; mains €22-28; ⊙1-4pm & 8pm-midnight Mon-Sat; Ⓜ Diagonal) is a clandestine restaurant lurking behind the Dry Martini (p105) bar. You will be shown a door through the open kitchen area to the 'storeroom', lined with hundreds of bottles of backlit, quality tipples. The menu has tempting options like the wild mushroom ravioli with langoustine or venison with puréed sweet potato.

Chicha Limoná
MEDITERRANEAN, PIZZERIA €€

14 Map p96, G1

Passeig de Sant Joan has become the newest haunt for the hussar-moustached, turned-up-cigarette-pants brigade, and bright, bustling Chicha Limoná has provided them with somewhere great to eat. Grilled octopus with quince jelly, pork with apple compote and pear tatin with crème anglaise are among the oft-changing dishes (set menu €12.90), along with homemade pizzas. (☏93 277 64 03; www. chichalimona.com; Passeig de Sant Joan 80; mains €10-16; ⊙8.30am-1am Tue-Thu, 8.30am-2am Fri, 9.30am-2am Sat, 9.30am-5pm Sun; 🛜; Ⓜ Tetuan)

Entrepanes Díaz
SANDWICHES €€

15 Map p96, D1

A new concept in upmarket gourmet sandwiches, from roast beef to suckling pig, along with sharing plates of Spanish specialties such as sea urchins and shrimp fritters, in a sparkling old-style bar. The policy of only hiring experienced waiters over 50 lends a certain gravitas to the operation and some especially charming service. (☏93 415 75 82; Carrer de Pau Claris 189; sandwiches €6-8, salads €12; ⊙11am-midnight Tue-Sat, 11am-6pm Sun; Ⓜ Diagonal)

Can Kenji
JAPANESE €€

16 Map p96, E1

If you want to go Japanese in Barcelona, this is the place. The chef of this understated little *izakaya* (the Japanese version of a tavern) gets his ingredients fresh from the city's markets, with traditional Japanese recipes receiving a Mediterranean touch. This is fusion at its very best. (☏93 476 18 23; www.cankenji. com; Carrer del Rosselló 325; mains €10-14; ⊙1-3.30pm & 8.30-11.30pm; Ⓜ Verdaguer)

Cata 1.81
TAPAS €€

17 Map p96, C4

A beautifully designed venue (with lots of small lights, some trapped in birdcages), this is the place to come for fine wines and dainty gourmet dishes like *raviolis amb bacallà* (salt-cod dumplings) or *truita de patates i tòfona negre* (thick potato tortilla with a delicate trace of black truffle).

Understand

Modernisme

In the late 19th century, Barcelona was booming and the city's culture of avant-garde experimentation was custom made for a group of outrageously talented architects who came to be known as Modernistas. Leading the way was Antoni Gaudí i Cornet (1852–1926). Gaudí personifies and largely transcends a movement that brought a thunderclap of innovative greatness to an otherwise middle-ranking European city.

The Style

Modernisme did not appear in isolation in Barcelona. To the British and French the style was art nouveau; the Germans called it Jugendstil (Youth Style). Whatever it was called, a key uniting element was the sensuous curve, implying movement, lightness and vitality. Modernista architects looked to the past for inspiration: Gothic, Islamic and Renaissance design in particular. At its most playful, Modernisme was able to intelligently flout the rule books of these styles and create exciting new cocktails.

The Architects

Gaudí and the two architects who most closely followed him in talent, Lluís Domènech i Montaner (1850–1923) and Josep Puig i Cadafalch (1867–1957), were Catalan nationalists. The political associations are significant, as Modernisme became a means of expression for Catalan identity; the style barely touched the rest of Spain. Gaudí took great inspiration from Gothic styles, but he also sought to emulate the harmony he observed in nature. Straight lines were out. The forms of plants and stones were in. Gaudí used complex string models weighted with plumb lines to make his calculations. The architect's work is at once a sublime reaching out to the heavens, and an earthy appeal to sinewy movement.

The Materials & Decoration

Stone, unclad brick, exposed iron and steel frames, and copious use of stained glass and ceramics in decoration, were all features of the new style. Modernista architects relied heavily on the skills of craftsmen who were the heirs of the guild masters and had absorbed centuries of knowhow about working with these materials. There were no concrete pours. Gaudí in particular relied on the old skills and even ran schools in La Sagrada Família workshops in a bid to keep them alive. Newer materials, such as forged iron, also came into their own during this period.

The best idea is to choose from one of several tasting-menu options. (☏ 93 323 68 18; www.cata181.com; Carrer de València 181; tapas €5.50-8; ☉ 6pm-midnight Mon-Sat; Ⓜ Passeig de Gràcia)

Taktika Berri
BASQUE, TAPAS €€

18 Map p96, C4

Get in early because the bar teems with punters from far and wide, anxious to wrap their mouths around some of the best Basque tapas in town. The hot morsels are all snapped up as soon as they arrive from the kitchen, so keep your eyes peeled. In the evening, it's all over by about 10.30pm. (☏ 93 453 47 59; Carrer de València 169; tapas from €3, mains €10-32; ☉ 1-4pm & 8.30-11pm Mon-Fri, 1-4pm Sat; ☏; Ⓜ Hospital Clínic)

Disfrutar
MODERN EUROPEAN €€€

19 Map p96, B4

In its first few months of life, Disfrutar rose stratospherically to become the city's finest restaurant – book now while it's still possible to get a table. Run by alumni of Ferran Adrià's game-changing El Bulli restaurant, it operates along similar lines. (☏ 93 348 68 96; www.en.disfrutarbarcelona.com; Carrer de Vilarroel 163; tasting menus €75/105/135; ☉ 1-4pm & 8-11pm Tue-Sat; Ⓜ Hospital Clínic)

Cinc Sentits
INTERNATIONAL €€€

20 Map p96, C4

Enter the realm of the 'Five Senses' to indulge in a jaw-dropping tasting menu consisting of a series of small, experimental dishes (there is no à la carte, although dishes can be tweaked to suit diners' requests). There is a lunch *menú* for €55. (☏ 93 323 94 90; www.cincsentits.com; Carrer d'Aribau 58; tasting menus €100/120; ☉ 1.30-3pm & 8.30-10pm Tue-Sat; Ⓜ Passeig de Gràcia)

Casa Calvet
CATALAN €€€

21 Map p96, G3

An early Gaudí masterpiece loaded with his trademark curvy features houses a swish restaurant (just to the right of the building's main entrance). Dress up and ask for an intimate *taula cabina* (wooden booth). You could opt for scallops and razor clams with pesto and buckwheat, or venison with juniper and porcini sauce. (☏ 93 412 40 12; www.casacalvet.es; Carrer de Casp 48; mains €28-31; ☉ 1-3.30pm & 8.30-11pm Mon-Sat; Ⓜ Urquinaona)

Drinking

Dry Martini BAR

22 Map p96, B2

Waiters with a discreetly knowing smile will attend to your cocktail needs and make uncannily good suggestions, but the house drink, taken at the bar or in one of the plush green leather banquettes, is a safe bet. The gin and tonic comes in an enormous mug-sized glass – one will take you most of the night. (📞93 217 50 80; www.drymartiniorg.com; Carrer d'Aribau 162-166; 🕑1pm-2.30am Mon-Thu, 6pm-3am Fri & Sat, 7pm-2.30am Sun; Ⓜ Diagonal)

Napar BCN BREWERY

23 Map p96, D4

The latest bar to open as part of Barcelona's burgeoning craft-beer scene, Napar has 12 beers on tap, six of which are beers brewed on-site, including a mix of IPAs, pale ale and stout. There's also an accomplished list of bottled beers. It's a stunning space, with a gleaming steampunk aesthetic, and serves some excellent food should hunger strike. (📞606 546467; www.naparbcn.com; Carrer de la Diputació 223; 🕑noon-midnight Tue-Thu, to 2am Fri & Sat, noon-5pm Sun; 📶; Ⓜ Universitat)

Antilla BCN CLUB

24 Map p96, B5

The salsateca in town, this is the place to come for Cuban *son,* merengue, salsa and a whole lot more. There are dance classes from around 8pm or 9pm from Tuesday to Friday. Check www.antillaescueladesalsa.com for details. (📞93 451 45 64; www.antillasalsa.com; Carrer d'Aragó 141; 🕑Wed-Thu free, Fri & Sat €10; 🕑10pm-5am Wed, 11pm-5am Thu, 11pm-6am Fri & Sat, 7pm-5am Sun; Ⓜ Urgell)

Milano COCKTAIL BAR

25 Map p96, E4

An absolute gem of hidden Barcelona nightlife, Milano is a subterranean old-school cocktail bar with velvet banquettes and glass-fronted cabinets, presided over by white-jacketed waiters, and completely invisible from street level. Check the website for details on occasional live music. (📞93 112 71 50; www.camparimilano.com; Ronda de la Universitat 35; 🕑noon-2.30am Mon-Sat, 6pm-2.30am Sun; Ⓜ Catalunya)

Les Gens Que J'Aime BAR

26 Map p96, E2

This intimate basement relic of the 1960s follows a deceptively simple formula: chilled jazz music in the background, minimal lighting from an

---

☑ Top Tip

The Gaixample

The area just above Gran Via de les Corts Catalanes and to the left of Rambla de Catalunya is popularly known as the 'Gaixample', for its proliferation of gay bars and restaurants. For listings, see p175.

assortment of flea-market lamps and a cosy, cramped scattering of red-velvet-backed lounges around tiny dark tables. (☎93 215 68 79; www.lesgensquejaime.com; Carrer de València 286; ⏱6pm-2.30am Sun-Thu, 7pm-3am Fri & Sat; Ⓜ Passeig de Gràcia)

City Hall
CLUB

27 🔊 Map p96, F4

A long corridor leads to the dance floor of this venerable and popular club, located in a former theatre. House and other electric sounds dominate, with occasional funk nights, and – on Sundays – a gay night, Black Room. Check the website for details. (☎93 238 07 22; www.cityhallbarcelona.com; Rambla de Catalunya 2-4; €10-15, incl 1 drink; ⏱midnight-5am Wed & Thu, midnight-6am Fri & Sat, 11pm-5am Sun; Ⓜ Catalunya)

Shopping

El Corte Inglés
DEPARTMENT STORE

28 🅐 Map p96, F4

This is now the city's only department store, with everything you'd expect, from computers to cushions, and high fashion to homewares. It's famous for its decent customer service (though this isn't always the case in Spain). El Corte Inglés has other branches, including at Portal de l'Àngel 19-21, Avinguda Diagonal 617, and Avinguda Diagonal 471-473 near Plaça de Francesc Macià. (☎93 306 38 00; www.elcorteingles.es; Plaça de Catalunya 14; ⏱9.30am-9.30pm Mon-Sat; Ⓜ Catalunya)

El Bulevard dels Antiquaris
ANTIQUES

29 🅐 Map p96, D3

More than 70 stores (be warned most close for lunch) are gathered under one roof (on the floor above the more general Bulevard Rosa arcade) to offer the most varied selection of collector's pieces. These range from old porcelain dolls through to fine crystal, from Asian antique furniture to old French goods, and from African and other ethnic art to jewellery. (☎93 215 44 99; www.bulevarddelsantiquaris.com; Passeig de Gràcia 55; ⏱10.30am-8.30pm Mon-Sat; Ⓜ Passeig de Gràcia)

Regia
BEAUTY

30 🅐 Map p96, E3

Reputed to be one of the best perfume stores in the city, and in business since 1928, Regia stocks all the name brands and also has a private perfume museum out the back. Aside from the range of perfumes, Regia sells all sorts of creams, lotions and colognes. It also has its own line of bath products. (☎93 216 01 21; www.regia.es; Passeig de Gràcia 39; ⏱9.30am-8.30pm Mon-Sat; Ⓜ Passeig de Gràcia)

Cubiña
HOMEWARES

31 🅐 Map p96, E1

Even if interior design doesn't ring your bell, it's worth a visit to this extensive temple to furniture, lamps and just about any home accessory your heart might desire, just to see this Domènech i Montaner building.

Spanish beer, Estrella Galicia

Admire the enormous and whimsical wrought-iron decoration at street level before heading inside to marvel at the ceiling, timber work, brick columns and windows. (☎93 476 57 21; www.cubinya.es; Carrer de Mallorca 291; ◷10am-2pm & 4.30-8.30pm Mon-Sat; MVerdaguer)

Adolfo Domínguez FASHION

32 🔒 Map p96, E3

One of the stars of Spanish prêt-à-porter, this label produces classic men's and women's garments from quality materials. Encompassing anything from regal party gowns to kids' outfits (that might have you thinking of British aristocracy), the broad range generally oozes a conservative air, with elegant cuts that make no concessions to rebellious urban ideals. (☎93 487 41 70; www.adolfodominguez.com; Passeig de Gràcia 32; ◷10am-9pm Mon-Sat; MPasseig de Gràcia)

Joan Múrria FOOD

33 🔒 Map p96, E2

Ramon Casas designed the century-old Modernista shop-front advertisements featured at this culinary temple. For a century the gluttonous have trembled at this altar of specialty food goods from around Catalonia and beyond. (☎93 215 57 89; www.murria.cat; Carrer de Roger de Llúria 85; ◷9am-2pm & 5-8pm Mon-Fri; MPasseig de Gràcia)

Top Sights
La Sagrada Família

Getting There

Ⓜ The easiest way to arrive, via Sagrada Família station (lines 2 and 5).

🚶 La Sagrada Família is a flat 1.5km walk from Passeig de Gràcia.

Spain's biggest tourist attraction and a work in progress for more than a century, La Sagrada Família is a unique, extraordinary piece of architecture. Conceived as a temple as atonement for Barcelona's sins of modernity, this giant church became Gaudí's holy mission. When completed it will have a capacity for 13,000 faithful and is, in medieval fashion, a work of storytelling art. Rich in religious iconography and symbolism, at once ancient and thoroughly modern, La Sagrada Família leaves no one unmoved.

Don't Miss

Nativity Facade

This astonishing tapestry in stone is, for now, the single most impressive feature of La Sagrada Família. Step back for an overall sense of this remarkable work, which was the first of the facades completed (in 1930), then draw near to examine the detail. It is replete with sculpted figures (Gaudí used plaster casts of local people as models) and images from nature.

Passion Facade

Symbolically facing the setting sun, the Passion facade – stripped bare and left to speak for itself – is the austere counterpoint to the Nativity facade's riotous decoration. From the Last Supper to his burial, Christ's story plays out in an S-shaped sequence from bottom to top. Check the cryptogram in which the numbers always add up to 33, Jesus' age at crucifixion.

A Hidden Portrait

Careful observation of the Passion facade will reveal a special tribute from sculptor Josep Subirachs to Gaudí. The central sculptural group (below Christ crucified) shows, from right to left, Christ bearing his cross, Veronica displaying the cloth with Christ's bloody image, a pair of soldiers, and watching it all, a man called the evangelist. Subirachs used a rare photo of Gaudí, taken a couple of years before his death, as the model for the evangelist's face.

Glory Facade

The Glory facade will be the most fanciful of them all, with a narthex boasting 16 hyperboloid lanterns topped by cones that will look something like an organ made of melting ice cream. Gaudí made only general drawings of the facade,

---

www.sagradafamilia.cat

Carrer de Mallorca 401

adult/concession/under 11
€15/13/free

⊙ 9am-8pm Apr-Sep, to 6pm Oct-Mar

Ⓜ Sagrada Família

☑ Top Tips

▶ Jump the queue by buying tickets online.

▶ Guided 50-minute tours are offered throughout the day. Alternatively, pick up an audioguide (75 minutes).

▶ For the complete experience, book a ticket that includes one of the towers.

▶ The best time to visit is at opening time on weekdays.

✕ Take a Break

It's not often we recommend Irish pubs, but **Michael Collins Pub** (☎ 93 459 19 64; www. michaelcollinspubs.com; Plaça de la Sagrada Família 4; ⊙ 1pm-2.30am Sun-Thu, 1pm-3am Fri & Sat; ☎; Ⓜ Sagrada Família) is an unusually authentic version of the genre, frequented by locals.

but its symbolism is clear: Christ in all his glory and the road to God.

The Interior & Apse

Inside, the roof is held up by a forest of extraordinary angled pillars. As the pillars soar towards the ceiling, they sprout a web of supporting branches, creating the effect of a forest canopy. The tree image is in no way fortuitous – Gaudí envisaged such an effect. Everything was thought through, including the shape and placement of windows to create the mottled effect one would see with sunlight pouring through the branches of a thick forest.

Columns & Stained Glass

The pillars are of four different types of stone. They vary in colour and load-bearing strength, from the soft Montjuïc stone pillars along the lateral aisles through to granite, dark grey basalt and finally burgundy-tinged Iranian porphyry for the key columns at the intersection of the nave and transept. The stained glass, divided in shades of red, blue, green and ochre, creates a hypnotic, magical atmosphere when the sun hits the windows.

Crypt

From the main apse, holes in the floor allow a view down into the crypt, which was the first part of the church to be completed in 1885. Built in a largely neo-Gothic style, it's here that Gaudí lies buried. The crypt has often been used as the main place of worship while the remainder of the church is completed.

La Sagrada Família

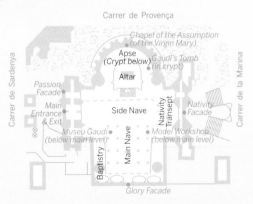

Carrer de Provença

Chapel of the Assumption (of the Virgin Mary)

Apse (Crypt below)

Gaudí's Tomb (in crypt)

Altar

Carrer de Sardenya

Passion Facade

Main Entrance & Exit

Museu Gaudí (below main level)

Side Nave

Nativity Transept

Nativity Facade

Model Workshop (below main level)

Carrer de la Marina

Baptistry

Main Nave

Glory Facade

Carrer de Mallorca

Bell Towers

The towers of the three facades represent the 12 Apostles (so far, eight have been built). Lifts whisk visitors up one tower of the Nativity and Passion facades (the latter gets longer queues) for marvellous views. There will eventually be 18 towers – 12 Apostles, four evangelists, the Virgin Mary and Christ – which when completed will make this the world's tallest church building.

Museu Gaudí

Jammed with old photos, drawings and restored plaster models that bring Gaudí's ambitions to life, the museum also houses an extraordinarily complex plumb-line device he used to calculate his constructions. It's like journeying through the mind of the great architect. Some of the models are upside down, as that's how Gaudí worked to best study the building's form and structural balance.

Nearby: Recinte Modernista de Sant Pau

A 500m walk north of La Sagrada Família, you'll find another masterpiece of Modernista style. Domènech i Montaner outdid himself as architect and philanthropist with the Hospital de la Santa Creu i de Sant Pau, redubbed in 2014 the Recinte Modernista de Sant Pau (p98). Domènech i Montaner wanted to create an environment that would also cheer up patients. Among artists who contributed statuary, ceramics and artwork was the prolific Eusebi Arnau. Among the highlights are the 16

Understand
Antoni Gaudí

Antoni Gaudí i Cornet (1852–1926) was born in Reus, trained initially in metalwork and obtained his architecture degree in 1878. Although part of the Modernista movement (p103), Gaudí had a style all his own. A recurring theme was his obsession with the harmony of natural forms. Straight lines are eliminated, and the lines between real and unreal, sober and dreamdrunk are all blurred. The grandeur of his vision was matched by an obsession with detail, as evidenced by his use of lifelike sculpture on the Nativity facade. With age he became almost exclusively motivated by stark religious conviction and from 1915 he gave up all other projects to devote himself exclusively to La Sagrada Família. When he died in June 1926 (he was knocked down by a tram on Gran Via de les Corts Catalanes) less than a quarter of La Sagrada Família had been completed. Under construction for over 130 years, the church's estimated completion date is 2026 at the earliest. As Gaudí is reported to have said when questioned about the never-ending project, 'My client is not in a hurry'.

lavishly decorated pavilions. Guided tours are available (adult/concession €16/11.20) in a variety of languages, upon request.

Local Life
Village Life in Gràcia

Getting There

Gràcia is a downhill walk from Park Güell.

Ⓜ Fontana station (line 3) or Joanic (line 4).

Ⓡ Take the suburban train from Catalunya station in the city centre to Gràcia station.

Located halfway between L'Eixample and Park Güell, Gràcia was a separate village until 1897, and its tight, narrow lanes and endless interlocking squares maintain a unique, almost village-like identity to this day. In places bohemian, in others rapidly gentrifying, Gràcia is Barcelona at its most eclectic, its nooks and crannies home to everything from amber lit old taverns to eco-minded boutiques.

1 Catalan Classic

A remnant from a bygone age, **Bar Bodega Quimet** (☎ 93 218 41 89; Carrer de Vic 23; tapas from €3; 🕑 2-11.30pm Mon-Fri, 1-11.30pm Sat & Sun; Ⓜ Fontana) is a delightfully atmospheric spot, with old bottles lining the walls, a burnished wooden bar and a seemingly exhaustive list of tapas.

2 Local Market

Built in the 1870s and covered in fizzy Modernista style in 1893, the **Mercat de la Llibertat** (☎ 93 217 09 95; www.mercatllibertat.com; Plaça de la Llibertat 27; 🕑 8am-8pm Mon-Fri, 8am-3pm Sat; ℞ FGC Gràcia) was designed by Francesc Berenguer i Mestres, Gaudí's long-time assistant.

3 Cruelty-Free Style

At **Amapola Vegan Shop** (☎ 93 010 62 73; www.amapolaveganshop.com; Travessera de Gràcia 129; 🕑 11am-2.30pm & 5-8.30pm Mon-Sat; Ⓜ Fontana or Diagonal), stylish clothing and accessories are all made from animal-free materials. You'll find sleek messenger bags, ballerina-style flats and cheeky T-shirts with slogans like 'Another Fucking Vegan' and 'No como mis amigos' (I don't eat my friends).

4 Retro Shopping

Doctor Paper (☎ 93 237 58 57; www.doctorpaperbcn.com; Travessera de Gràcia 130; 🕑 10.30am-2pm & 5-8.30pm Mon-Sat; ℞ FGC Gràcia) is a fun little shop full of whimsical objects and retro crafts. Wind-up robots, make-your-own-airplane kits, vintage postcards and painted enamel cups are all part of the treasure trove.

5 Gift Ideas

Magnesia (☎ 93 119 01 87; www.magnesiabcn.com; Carrer del Torrent de l'Olla 192; 🕑 10.30am-2pm & 4.30-8pm Mon-Fri, 10.30am-2pm Sat; Ⓜ Lesseps or Fontana) is a petite store so packed with intrigue that you might want to just giftwrap the whole thing. There is fairytale-esque stationery, framed illustrations, statement-piece jewellery, ceramics and old-fashioned looking toys.

6 Plaça de la Virreina

Thanks to the low-slung houses along one side and the 17th-century Església de Sant Joan on the other, Plaça de la Virreina is one of the most village-like of Gràcia's squares. With its outdoor tables, it's a lively hub for locals.

7 Local Bar

Bar Canigò (☎ 93 213 30 49; Carrer de Verdi 2; 🕑 10am-2am Mon-Fri, 8pm-3am Sat; Ⓜ Fontana) is a corner bar on an animated square and a timeless locals' spot to sip a beer and chat. It's especially welcoming in winter.

8 Cafe Culture

La Nena (☎ 93 285 14 76; www.chocolaterialanena.com; Carrer de Ramón y Cajal 36; desserts from €4.50; 🕑 9am-10pm; 🚼; Ⓜ Fontana) is a neighbourhood favourite for its *suïssos* (hot chocolate) and *melindros* (spongy sweet biscuits). The area out the back is designed to keep kids busy, with toys, books and a blackboard.

Top Sights
Park Güell

Getting There

Ⓜ The walk to the park is signposted from both Vallcarca and Lesseps stations (both line 3).

🚌 24 drops you at an entrance near the top of the park.

One of Antoni Gaudí's best-loved creations, Park Güell – a fantasy public park that was designed as a gated playground for Barcelona's rich – climbs a hillside north of the centre. This is where the master architect turned his hand to landscape gardening and the result is an expansive and playful stand of greenery interspersed with otherworldly structures glittering with ceramic tiles. The lasting impression is of a place where the artificial almost seems more natural than the natural.

El Drac (the Dragon), Park Güell

Don't Miss

Stairway & Sala Hipóstila

The steps up from the entrance and the two Hansel and Gretel–style gatehouses are a mosaic of fountains, ancient Catalan symbols and a much photographed dragon-lizard. Atop the stairs is the Sala Hipóstila, a forest of 86 Doric columns (some of them leaning at an angle and all inspired by ancient Greece); the space was intended as a market.

Banc de Trencadís

Atop the Sala Hipóstila is a broad open space; its highlight is the Banc de Trencadís, a tiled bench curving sinuously around the perimeter and alternately interpreted as a mythical serpent or, typically for Gaudí, waves in the sea. Although Gaudí was responsible for the form, the *trencadís* (broken tile) surface designs were the work of Gaudí's right-hand man, Josep Maria Jujol.

Casa-Museu Gaudí

The spired house east of the Banc de Trencadís is the **Casa-Museu Gaudí** (www.casamuseugaudi.org; adult/student/child €5.50/4.50/free; ⏱9am-8pm Apr-Sep, 10am-6pm Oct-Mar), where Gaudí lived for most of his last 20 years (1906–26). It contains furniture by him and other memorabilia, and its muted interior is a curious contrast to the extravagance of so many of the structures he designed.

The Viaducts

Much of the park's eastern end is dominated by the viaducts, which were Gaudí's solution to the problem of getting people and vehicles (not water) into the park. Slanting columns and local stone create an astonishing effect, seeming to spring from a fairy tale and creating the illusion that the whole structure was carved out of the mountain itself.

---

www.parkguell.cat

Carrer d'Olot 7

admission to central area adult/child €8/6

⏱8am-9.30pm May-Aug, to 8pm Sep-Apr

🚌24, 32, Ⓜ Lesseps or Vallcarca

☑ Top Tips

▶ If travelling by metro, Vallcarca station is better for arriving (the uphill trek to the park is eased by escalators); Lesseps is better for leaving (it's downhill all the way).

▶ Study the details: crockery pieces adorn some sections of the Banc de Trencadís.

▶ Arrive early on weekdays and avoid weekends in summer.

✗ Take a Break

Before or after making the trip up to the park, stop off at **La Panxa del Bisbe** (☎93 213 70 49; Carrer del Torrent de les Flors 156; tapas €8-14, tasting menus from €30; ⏱1.30-3.30pm & 8.30pm-midnight Tue-Sat; Ⓜ Joanic) for deliciously creative tapas and good wines.

Explore

Montjuïc, Poble Sec & Sant Antoni

Looming above sea and city, Montjuïc is a lovely stand of lawns and gardens interspersed with wonderful museums and sites that took centre stage during the 1992 Olympics. At the foot of the hill lies Poble Sec, its tightly packed streets home to buzzing bars and tapas haunts. The dining and nightlife scene continues in Sant Antoni, just across Avinguda del Paral·lel.

The Sights in a Day

☀️ Before we get started, a word of warning: dining options on the hill are limited and overpriced, so pack a picnic lunch from the **Mercat de la Boqueria** (p46). However you get here – we suggest the **Teleférico del Puerto** (p82) cable car from Barceloneta – start at the summit and work your way down. The **Castell de Montjuïc** (p128) promises marvellous views, as do the **Jardins del Mirador** (p130). Visit the **Fundació Joan Miró** (p122) before finding a quiet corner of the **Jardins de Mossèn Cinto de Verdaguer** (p130) for lunch.

☀️ Take a peak at Barcelona's Olympic moment at **L'Anella Olímpica & Estadi Olímpic** (p129), then spend the rest of the afternoon exploring Catalan treasures at the renowned **Museu Nacional d'Art de Catalunya** (p118). Even if you don't have time to go inside, take a peak at **CaixaForum** (p128), housed in an eye-catching Modernista building.

🌙 Stay long enough to catch the **Font Màgica** (pictured left; p129) before heading on to **Quimet i Quimet** (p132) for delicious tapas and **Fàbrica Moritz** (p132) for cold brews. End the night back up on Montjuïc with magical views over drinks at **La Caseta del Migdia** (p133) or dancing at **La Ter-rrazza** (p133).

For a local's night out in Sant Antoni and Poble Sec, see p124.

👁 Top Sights

Museu Nacional d'Art de Catalunya (p118)

Fundació Joan Miró (p122)

◯ Local Life

Nightlife in Sant Antoni & Poble Sec (p124)

💜 Best of Barcelona

Museums, Art & Design

Museu Nacional d'Art de Catalunya (p118)

Fundació Joan Miró (p122)

CaixaForum (p128)

Tapas

Tickets (p132)

Quimet i Quimet (p132)

Bar Ramón (p125)

Getting There

Ⓜ **Metro** Paral·lel station (lines 2 and 3), then funicular (9am to 10pm) to Estació Parc Montjuïc, where a cable car heads higher.

🚌 **Bus** Bus 50, 55 and 61, or No 193 from Plaça d'Espanya to the *castell* (castle).

Cable Car Teleférico del Puerto from Torre de Sant Sebastiá in Barceloneta to Montjuïc.

Top Sights
Museu Nacional d'Art de Catalunya

Barcelona's finest art collection looks out over the city from the Palau Nacional, the pompous centrepiece of the 1929 World Exhibition. The rich collection commences with a breathtaking selection of Romanesque art from the Catalan Pyrenees, and ends with works by Picasso and Dalí, with lavish detours into Gothic, Renaissance and baroque styles en route. Although there are many remarkable artworks here, it's the sheer breadth and scale of the collection that lives longest in the memory.

Map p126, C3

www.museunacional.cat

Mirador del Palau Nacional

adult/student/child €12/8.40/free, after 3pm Sat & 1st Sun of month free

⊙10am-8pm Tue-Sat, to 3pm Sun May-Sep, to 6pm Tue-Sat Oct-Apr

Ⓜ Espanya

The Four Columns by Josep Puig i Cadafalch in front of Museu Nacional d'Art de Catalunya

Don't Miss

Romanesque Frescoes

The beautifully displayed Romanesque art section constitutes one of Europe's greatest such collections. It consists mainly of 11th- and 12th-century frescoes from churches in the Catalan Pyrenees. While it's all exceptional, the two outstanding collections are the Església de Sant Climent de Taüll frescoes (Room 7) and the Església de Santa Maria de Taüll frescoes (Room 9).

Gothic Collection

Lovers of medieval religious art will want to linger over the ground-floor display of Gothic art, which is dominated by deeply textured altarpieces and other works, including paintings by Catalan painters Bernat Martorell and Jaume Huguet. Amid it all, seek out the sculpture *Head of Christ* by Jaume Cascalls, a haunting bust dating from 1352.

El Greco & Fra Angelico

Before leaving the Gothic centuries and heading upstairs, two paintings warrant close and prolonged inspection. The first is *Saint Peter and Saint Paul* (1595–1600) by Doménikos Theotokópoulos, better known as El Greco. The second work is the *Madonna of Humility* (1433–35) by Fra Angelico, an idealised, near-perfect counterpoint to El Greco's slender, elongated figures.

Spanish Masters

After passing through the soaring auditorium, climb to the 1st floor, where the masters of 17th-century Spanish art make a brief appearance. Francisco de Zurbarán's *Immaculate Conception* (1632) looks out across Room 39 at his strangely disconcerting *Saint Francis of Assisi*. Nearby, Room 41 is shared by Josep de Ribera and the masterful *Saint Paul* by Velázquez (1619).

☑ Top Tips

▶ If you're visiting more Barcelona museums, consider buying the Articket BCN (p52), which gives admission to this and five other museums for €30.

▶ Be sure to take in the fine view from the terrace just in front of the museum. It draws crowds around sunset.

▶ Another fine viewpoint is on the museum's roof terrace, where drinks are available.

✖ Take a Break

There's a casual cafe on the main level for drinks, sandwiches and desserts.

On the upper level, the beautifully set **Oleum** (Museu Nacional d'Art de Catalunya (MNAC), Mirador del Palau Nacional; mains €18-27; ⏱12.30-4pm Tue-Sat & 8.30-11.30pm Fri & Sat) serves pricey, high-end Mediterranean fare, with great views over the city.

Museu Nacional d'Art de Catalunya

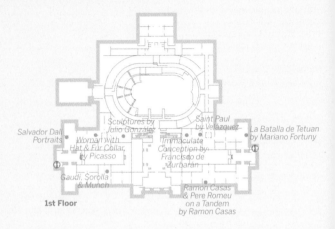

Salvador Dalí Portraits

Sculptures by Julio Gonzalez

Saint Paul by Velázquez

La Batalla de Tetuan by Mariano Fortuny

Woman with Hat & Fur Collar by Picasso

Immaculate Conception by Francisco de Zurbarán

Gaudí, Sorolla & Munch

Ramon Casas & Pere Romeu on a Tandem by Ramon Casas

1st Floor

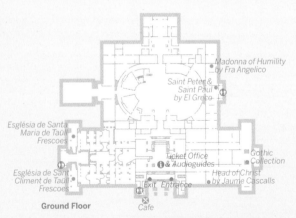

Madonna of Humility by Fra Angelico

Saint Peter & Saint Paul by El Greco

Església de Santa Maria de Taüll Frescoes

Gothic Collection

Ticket Office & Audioguides

Església de Sant Climent de Taüll Frescoes

Head of Christ by Jaume Cascalls

Exit Entrance

Ground Floor

Café

Catalan Masters

The 1st floor is dominated by Catalan painters and offers an intriguing insight into artists little known beyond Catalonia. There's much to turn the head, but our highlights are Mariano Fortuny's *La Batalla de Tetuan* (1863–73) and the works of Modernista painter Ramon Casas (1866–1932), especially *Ramon Casas and Pere Romeu on a Tandem* (1897).

Gaudí, Sorolla & Munch

Some furniture pieces by Antoni Gaudí and Joaquim Mir (1873–1940) continue the Catalan theme – the latter's *Terraced Village* (1909) is a lovely work. But dropped down amid this relatively uniform collection of Catalan art are two works by undoubted European masters: Valencian painter Joaquín Sorolla and Norwegian Edvard Munch.

Picasso & Dalí

Two sober works by Salvador Dalí – *Portrait of my Father* (1925) and *Portrait of Joan Maria Torres* (1921) – are what everyone comes to see, but fans of Picasso are rewarded by a handful of paintings, among them the cubist *Woman with Hat and Fur Collar* (1937), which is one of the museum's standout pieces.

FOTOKON/SHUTTERSTOCK ©

Sculpture at the Museu Nacional d'Art de Catalunya

Julio González

Having checked off the big names, most visitors head for the exit, but we recommend you stay long enough to appreciate the beautiful sculptures by Julio González (1876–1942), Catalonia's premier 20th-century sculptor. His abstract human forms, such as those in *Still Life II* (1929), have a slender grace.

Top Sights
Fundació Joan Miró

Dedicated to one of the greatest artists to emerge in Barcelona in the 20th century, Joan Miró (1893–1983), this outstanding gallery is a must-see. The foundation holds the greatest single collection of the artist's work, comprising around 220 of his paintings, 180 sculptures, some textiles and more than 8000 drawings. Only a smallish portion is ever on display, but there's always a representative sample from his early paintings through to a master in full command of his unique style.

👁 Map p126, E3

www.fmirobcn.org

Parc de Montjuïc

adult/child €12/free

🕙10am-8pm Tue-Sat, to 9pm Thu, to 2.30pm Sun & holidays

🚌 55, 150, 🚇 Paral·lel

Fundació Joan Miró by architect Josep Lluís Sert

Don't Miss

The Formative Years

Room 16 The young Joan Miró began, like most masters, by painting figurative forms, but his move to Paris in 1920 prompted a shift to the avant-garde styles that he would make his own. His 1925 work *Painting (The White Glove)* has that unmistakable Miró sense of the artist having taken everything apart and reassembled it on a whim.

The War Years

Room 17 Miró spent most of the Spanish Civil War (1936–39) in exile in France, and his works from this period are uncharacteristically dark. During WWII, his approach to painting changed, reflecting a desire to escape reality, as highlighted in the bold colours and childlike figures of *The Morning Star* (1940) and *Woman Dreaming of Escape* (1945).

1960s & Paper

Rooms 19 & 20 After soaking up the vivid colours of Miró's 1960s paintings in Room 19 – linger over *Painting (for Emil Fernandez Miró)* from 1963 and *Catalan Peasant in the Moonlight* (1968) in particular – pause in Room 20. This is where Miró's love of painting on paper, and the flexibility it offered, is showcased with paintings that span five decades.

Col·lecció Katsuta

Rooms 21 & 22 This far-reaching private collection of Miró's works feels like an unexpected bonus at exhibition's end. It's a reprise of his career from the sober Catalan landscapes of his youth (such as *Landscape, Mont-Roig* in Room 21) through to the masterful and enigmatic *The Smile of a Tear* (1973) in Room 22.

☑ Top Tips

▶ For the full experience, pay the extra €5 for the multimedia guide, which includes commentary on major works, additional info on Miró's life and work, and images and photographs.

▶ Arrive at opening times for the smallest crowds.

▶ Head to the gardens just downhill from the museum for a scenic stroll after visiting the galleries.

✗ Take a Break

Near the centre of the museum, a pleasant light-filled restaurant serves freshly prepared Mediterranean dishes. The adjoining outdoor terrace is also a fine spot for a drink.

A short walk from the museum (head right when exiting), **La Font del Gat** (Map p126, D3; ☏ 93 289 04 04; www. lafontdelgat.com; Passeig de Santa Madrona 28; mains €16-21; ⏰ 10am-6pm Tue-Fri, from noon Sat & Sun) has high-end Catalan cuisine with outdoor dining on the terrace.

Local Life
Nightlife in Sant Antoni & Poble Sec

For locals, the area of Poble Sec and neighbouring Sant Antoni is the hot destination of the moment, with a buzzing array of cafes, bars and eateries drawing young, hip crowds to this once sleepy corner of Barcelona. This route starts off with some tapas bar snacking, before moving on to more serious drinking dens and nightspots.

❶ Culinary Superstar

One of Albert Adrià's first-rate eating spots, **Bodega 1900** (☑ 93 325 26 59; www.bodega1900.com; Carrer de Tamarit 91; tapas €5-14; ⊙ noon-4pm & 7-11.30pm; Ⓜ Sant Antoni) mimics an old-school tapas bar, but this is no ordinary spit-and-sawdust joint. Witness, for example, the simply exquisite *mollete de calamars*, served piping hot from the oven with chipotle mayonnaise, kim chi and lemon zest.

❷ Tapas & Rock 'n' Roll

Near the Mercat de Sant Antoni, **Bar Ramón** (☎ 93 325 02 83; www.barramon. com; Carrer del Comte Borrell 81; tapas €5-12; ⏰ 8.30pm-midnight Mon-Sat & 9am-4pm Fri & Sat; Ⓜ Sant Antoni) is a much-loved joint (opened in the 1930s) that serves up superb tapas plates. Calamari, meatballs, stuffed mushrooms, octopus – you can't go wrong.

❸ Aussie Style

On a stretch that now teems with cafes, Australian-run **Federal** (☎ 93 187 36 07; www.federalcafe.es; Carrer del Parlament 39; mains €9-12; ⏰ 8am-11pm Mon-Thu, 8am-1am Fri, 9am-1am Sat, 9am-5.30pm Sun; 🛜🚼; Ⓜ Sant Antoni) was the trailbazer, with its breezy atmosphere and superb brunches. Alongside healthy, tasty meals, cupcakes and good coffee are available all day.

❹ Terrace Drinks

It bills itself as a wine bar, but actually the wine selection at **Bar Calders** (☎ 93 329 93 49; Carrer del Parlament 25; ⏰ 5pm-2am Mon-Fri, 11am-2.30am Sat, 11am-midnight Sun; Ⓜ Sant Antoni) is its weak point. As an all-day cafe and tapas bar, however, it's unbeatable. With a few tables outside on a tiny pedestrian side-street, this has become the favoured meeting point for the neighbourhood's boho element.

❺ Atmospheric Den

A succession of nooks and crannies, dotted with flea-market finds and dimly lit in violets, reds and yellows, make **Tinta Roja** (☎ 93 443 32 43; www.tintaroja.

cat; Carrer de la Creu dels Molers 17; ⏰ 8.30pm-1am Wed, to 2am Thu, to 3am Fri & Sat; Ⓜ Poble Sec) an intimate spot for a drink and an occasional show in the back.

❻ Air of Decadence

Seduction is the word that springs to mind in **El Rouge** (☎ 666 251556; Carrer del Poeta Cabanyes 21; ⏰ 11pm-2am Mon, 8pm-2am Tue & Thu, 10pm-3am Fri & Sat; 🛜; Ⓜ Poble Sec), a bordello-red lounge cocktail bar. The walls are laden with heavy-framed paintings, dim lamps and mirrors, and no two chairs are alike. It has many cultural events: poetry readings, theatrical shows, art exhibitions.

❼ Bohemian Bodega

At **Gran Bodega Saltó** (☎ 93 441 37 09; www.bodegasalto.net; Carrer de Blesa 36; ⏰ 7pm-2am Mon-Thu, noon-3am Fri & Sat, noon-midnight Sun; Ⓜ Paral·lel) the ranks of barrels give away the bar's history as a traditional bodega. Now, after a little psychedelic redecoration with odd lamps, figurines and old Chinese beer ads, it's a magnet for an eclectic barfly crowd that can get pretty lively on nights when there is live music.

❽ Dance-Hall Finale

The iconic **Sala Apolo** (☎ 93 441 40 01; www.sala-apolo.com; Carrer Nou de la Rambla 113; club €12-18, concerts vary; ⏰ 12.30am-5am Mon-Thu, 12.30am-6am Fri & Sat; Ⓜ Paral·lel) is a fine old theatre, where red velvet dominates and you feel as though you're in a movie-set dance-hall scene. There are concerts earlier in the evening, with DJs kicking things off after midnight.

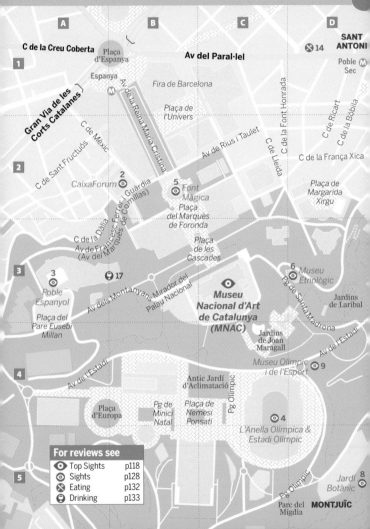

A | B | C | D

1

C de la Creu Coberta

Plaça d'Espanya

Av del Paral·lel

SANT ANTONI

✕ 14

Poble Ⓜ Sec

Espanya Ⓜ

Fira de Barcelona

Av de la Reina Maria Cristina

Plaça de l'Univers

C de la Font Honrada

C de Ricart

C de la Bòbila

Gran Via de les Corts Catalanes

C de Mèxic

2

C de Sant Fructuós

Av de Rius i Taulet

C de Lleida

C de la França Xica

CaixaForum ◉ 2

Av de Francesc Ferrer i Guàrdia (Av del Marquès de Comillas)

5 ◉ Font Màgica

Plaça de Margarida Xirgu

Plaça del Marquès de Foronda

C de la Dàlia

Plaça de les Cascades

3

3 ◉ Poble Espanyol

⛪ 17

Av dels Montanyans

Mirador del Palau Nacional

◉ **Museu Nacional d'Art de Catalunya (MNAC)**

6 ◉ Museu Etnològic

Pg de Santa Madrona

Jardins de Laribal

Plaça del Pare Eusebi Millan

Jardins de Joan Maragall

Av de l'Estadi

Museu Olímpic i de l'Esport ◉ 9

4

Av de l'Estadi

Plaça d'Europa

Pg de Minici Natal

Antic Jardí d'Aclimatació

Plaça de Nemesi Ponsati

Pg Olímpic

4 ◉

L'Anella Olímpica & Estadi Olímpic

5

Pg Olímpic

Jardí Botànic 8 ◉

Parc del Migdia

MONTJUÏC

E **F** 16 **G** **H**

16 ⊙ ⊗ 13 ⬆ N 0 ——— 400 m
                    0 ——— 0.2 miles

Av del Paral·lel

Ⓜ Paral·lel

Parc de
les Tres
Xemeneies

C de la Concòrdia
C de Blasco de Garay
C de Margarit
C de Blai ⊗11
POBLE
SEC
C de Radas
C de la Creu dels Molers
C de Tapioles
C del Poeta Cabanyes
C de Salvà
C del Roser
C de la Fontrodona
C Nou de la Rambla
10 ⊗
C de Blesa
C de Cabanes
C de Vila i Vilà
C de Piquer
C de Palaudàries

Plaça
del
Sortidor
C d'Anníbal
Pg de l'Exposició

Pg de Montjuïc

7 ⊙ MUHBA
Refugi 307

Transbordador
Aeri (Miramar)

Pg de la Font Trobada

Plaça de
Carlos
Ibáñez

Plaça de
l'Armada

Pg de Miramar

Av de Miramar

C de Montjuïc

rdí de les
scultures
undació
oan Miró
⊙
aça
Neptu

Av de Miramar

Estació ⊙
Parc
Montjuïc

Plaça
de Dante

Jardins de
Joan Brossa

Jardins
de Miramar

Jardins de
Mossèn Costa
i Llobera

dels
es Pins

Jardins de
Mossèn Cinto
de Verdaguer

Plaça de
la Sardana

Estació ⊙
Mirador

C del Doctor Font i Quer

Jardins
del
Mirador

Carretera de Miramar

Carretera de Miramar

Camí Baix del Castell

C de Montjuïc

Pg del Migdia

Av del Castell

Castell ⊙

Ronda del Litoral

Ⓜ Estació
del Port

Moll
de la
Costa

C de la Cartoixa

Castell de
Montjuïc ⊙1

15
⊙

Camí del Mar

Sights

Castell de Montjuïc

FORTRESS, GARDENS

1 ◎ Map p126, F5

This forbidding *castell* (castle or fort) dominates the southeastern heights of Montjuïc and enjoys commanding views over the Mediterranean. It dates, in its present form, from the late 17th and 18th centuries. For most of its dark history, it has been used to watch over the city and as a political prison and killing ground. (📞93 256 44 45; www.bcn.cat/castelldemontjuic; Carretera de Montjuïc 66; adult/child €5/free, after 3pm Sun free; ⏰10am-8pm Apr-Oct, to 6pm Nov-Mar; 🚌150, Telefèric de Montjuïc, Castell de Montjuïc)

CaixaForum

GALLERY

2 ◎ Map p126, B2

The Caixa building society prides itself on its involvement in (and ownership of) art, in particular all that is contemporary. Its premier art expo space in Barcelona hosts part of the bank's extensive collection from around the globe. The setting is a completely renovated former factory, the Fàbrica Casaramona, an outstanding Modernista brick structure designed by Puig i Cadafalch. From 1940 to 1993 it housed the First Squadron of the police cavalry unit – 120 horses in all. (📞93 476 86 00; www.fundacio.lacaixa.es; Avinguda de Francesc Ferrer i Guàrdia 6-8; adult/student & child €4/free, 1st Sun of month free; ⏰10am-8pm; 🅿; Ⓜ Espanya)

Poble Espanyol

CULTURAL CENTRE

3 ◎ Map p126, A3

Welcome to Spain! All of it! This 'Spanish Village' is both a cheesy souvenir hunters' haunt and an intriguing scrapbook of Spanish architecture built for the Spanish crafts section of the 1929 World Exhibition. You can meander from Andalucía to the Balearic Islands in the space of a couple of hours, visiting surprisingly good copies of Spain's characteristic buildings. (www.poble-espanyol.com;

Top Tip

Travel by Cable Car

The fastest way to get from Barceloneta to Montjuïc is aboard the **Teleférico del Puerto** (www.telefericodebarcelona.com; Av de Miramar, Jardins de Miramar; one way/return €11/16.50; ⏰11am-7pm Mar-Oct, to 5:30pm Nov-Feb; 🚌50, 153), which offers sublime views of sea and city. On Montjuïc, another cable car, the **Telefèric de Montjuïc** (www.telefericdemontjuic.cat; Av de Miramar 30; adult/child one way €8/6.20; ⏰10am-9pm Jun-Sep, to 7pm Oct-May; 🚌55, 150), runs from Estació Parc Montjuïc to the Castell de Montjuïc. The two cable-car stations are roughly 1.3km from each other. You can also reach the Telefèric de Montjuïc via the **funicular railway** that runs from the metro at the Paral·lel stop and is part of the metro fare system.

CATARINA BELOVA/SHUTTERSTOCK ©

Poble Espanyol

Avinguda de Francesc Ferrer i Guàrdia 13; adult/child €12/7; ⊙9am-8pm Mon, to midnight Tue-Thu & Sun, to 3am Fri & Sat; 🚍13, 23, 150, Ⓜ Espanya)

L'Anella Olímpica & Estadi Olímpic

OLYMPIC SITE

4 ◉ Map p126, C4

L'Anella Olímpica (Olympic Ring) is the group of installations built for the main events of the 1992 Olympics. They include the **Piscines Bernat Picornell**, where the swimming and diving events were held, and the surprisingly small 65,000-capacity Estadi Olímpic, which is open to the public when it's not in use for sporting events or concerts. (www.estadiolimpic. cat; Avinguda de l'Estadi; admission free; ⊙8am-8pm Apr-Sep, 10am-6pm Oct-Mar; 🚍50, 61, 150)

Font Màgica

FOUNTAIN

5 ◉ Map p126, B2

A huge fountain that crowns the long sweep of the Avinguda de la Reina Maria Cristina to the grand facade of the Palau Nacional, Font Màgica is a unique performance in which the water can look like seething fireworks or a mystical cauldron of colour. (📞93 316 10 00; Avinguda de la Reina Maria Cristina; ⊙every 30min 7-9pm Fri & Sat Nov-Mar, 9.30-11pm Thu-Sun Apr-Oct; Ⓜ Espanya)

Local Life
Garden Strolls

The **Jardins del Mirador** (Map p126, G4; ⊙10am-sunset; cable car Telefèric de Montjuïc, Mirador) offer fine views over the port of Barcelona. Further downhill, the **Jardins de Mossèn Costa i Llobera** (Map p126, H3) are of particular interest for their collection of tropical and desert plants – including a forest of cacti. The beautiful, cool **Jardins de Mossèn Cinto de Verdaguer** (Map p126, F3; www.bcn.cat/parcsijardins; ⊙10am-sunset; ☐55, 150) are devoted to bulbs and aquatic plants.

Museu Etnològic   MUSEUM

6 ◎ Map p126, D3

Barcelona's ethnology museum presents an intriguing permanent collection that delves into the rich heritage of Catalonia. Exhibits cover origin myths, religious festivals, folklore, and the blending of the sacred and the secular (along those lines, don't miss the Nativity scene with that quirky Catalan character *el caganer*, aka 'the crapper'). (www.museuetnologic.bcn.cat; Passeig de Santa Madrona 16-22; adult/child €5/3; ⊙10am-7pm Tue-Sat, to 8pm Sun; ☐55)

MUHBA Refugi 307   HISTORIC SITE

7 ◎ Map p126, G2

Part of the Museu d'Història de Barcelona (MUHBA), this is a shelter that dates back to the days of the Spanish Civil War. Barcelona was the city most heavily bombed from the air during the civil war and had more than 1300 air-raid shelters. Local citizens started digging this one under a fold of Montjuïc in March 1937. It's open on Sundays by tour only. (☎93 256 21 22; www.museuhistoria.bcn.cat; Carrer Nou de la Rambla 169; adult/child incl tour €3.40/free; ⊙tours 10.30am, 11.30am & 2.30pm Sun; Ⓜ Paral·lel)

Jardí Botànic   GARDENS

8 ◎ Map p126, D5

This botanical garden is dedicated to Mediterranean flora and has a collection of some 40,000 plants and 1500 species that thrive in areas with a climate similar to that of the Mediterranean, such as the Eastern Mediterranean, Spain (including the Balearic and Canary Islands), North Africa, Australia, California, Chile and South Africa. (www.museuciencies.cat; Carrer del Doctor Font i Quer 2; adult/child €3.50/free, after 3pm Sun free; ⊙10am-7pm Apr-Sep, to 5pm Oct-Mar; ☐55, 150)

Museu Olímpic i de l'Esport   MUSEUM

9 ◎ Map p126, D4

This information-packed interactive museum is dedicated to the history of sport and the Olympic Games. After picking up tickets, you wander down a ramp that snakes below ground level and is lined with displays on the history of sport, starting with the ancients. (☎93 292 53 79; www.museuolimpicbcn.com; Avinguda de l'Estadi 60; adult/student €5.10/3.20; ⊙10am-8pm Tue-Sat, 10am-2.30pm Sun; ☐55, 150)

Understand

Twentieth-Century Masters

Spain, and Catalonia in particular, produced an astonishing number of world-renowned 20th-century painters, but three stand high above the rest: Pablo Picasso, Salvador Dalí and Joan Miró.

Pablo Picasso

Born in Málaga in southern Spain, Pablo Ruiz Picasso (1881–1973) moved with his family to Barcelona in 1895. Despite spending much of his later life away from the city he returned often, and frequently said he considered Barcelona to be his true home. Picasso must have been one of the most restless artists of all time. His work underwent repeated revolutions as he passed from one creative phase to another – from his gloomy Blue Period, through the brighter Rose Period, and by the mid-1920s to dabbling with surrealism. Picasso went on to become the master of cubism, inspired by his fascination with primitivism, such as that of African masks and early Iberian sculpture. View a fine selection of his early works in Barcelona's Museu Picasso (p58).

Salvador Dalí

Separated from Picasso by barely a generation, Salvador Dalí (1904–89) started off dabbling in cubism, but quickly became identified with the surrealists. This complex character's 'hand-painted dream photographs', as he called them, are virtuoso executions brimming with detail and nightmare images dragged up from a feverish and Freud-fed imagination. Preoccupied with Picasso's fame, Dalí built himself a reputation as an outrageous showman and self-promoter. A frequent visitor to Barcelona, he was born in Figueres and spent much of his life in the seaside village of Cadaqués.

Joan Miró

Barcelona-born Joan Miró (1893–1983) developed a joyous and childlike style that earned him the epithet 'the most surrealist of us all' from the French writer André Breton. His later and best-known period is characterised by the simple use of bright colours and forms in combinations of symbols that represented women, birds (the link between earth and the heavens), stars (the unattainable heavenly world and source of imagination) and a sort of net that entraps all these levels of the cosmos. The Fundació Joan Miró (p122) houses the most complete collection of his work.

Eating

Palo Cortao

TAPAS €€

10 Map p126, G2

Palo Cortao has a solid reputation for its beautifully executed seafood and meat dishes, served at fair prices. Highlights include octopus with white bean hummus, skirt steak with foie armagnac, and tuna tataki tempura. You can order half sizes of all plates – which will allow you to try more dishes. (📞93 188 90 67; www.palocortao. es; Carrer de Nou de la Rambla 14; mains €10-15; ⏰8pm-1am Tue-Sun & 1-5pm Sat & Sun; Ⓜ Paral·lel)

Quimet i Quimet

TAPAS €€

11 Map p126, F1

Quimet i Quimet is a family-run business that has been passed down from generation to generation. There's barely space to swing a *calamar* in this bottle-lined, standing-room-only place, but it is a treat for the palate, with *montaditos* (tapas on a slice of bread) made to order. (📞93 442 31 42; Carrer del Poeta Cabanyes 25; tapas €4-10, montaditos around €3; ⏰noon-4pm & 7-10.30pm Mon-Fri, noon-4pm Sat; Ⓜ Paral·lel)

Casa Xica

FUSION €€

12 Map p126, D2

On the parlour floor of an old house, Casa Xica is a casual but artfully designed space that fuses elements of the Far East with fresh Catalan ingredients (owners Marc and Raquel lived

Local Life

Culinary Lane

The pedestrianised **Carrer de Blai** (Map p126, F1) is a great place to wander in the evening. You'll find a wide range of tapas bars, cafes and restaurants, with outdoor tables on the lane. Beer-and-tapas specials in the early evening draw a jovial crowd.

and travelled in Asia). (📞93 600 58 58; Carrer de la França Xica 20; sharing plates €9-15; ⏰1.30-3pm & 8.30-11.30pm Mon-Sat; Ⓜ Poble Sec)

Fàbrica Moritz

CATALAN €€

13 Map p126, G1

With the help of architect Jean Nouvel and chef Jordi Vilà, this microbrewery from the people behind Moritz beer has been rebuilt and opened with great fanfare as a vast food and drink complex, with wine bar and restaurant. The tapas and more substantial dishes comprise all the cornerstones of Catalan cuisine and plenty more, but be prepared to queue. (📞93 426 00 50; www.moritz.com; Ronda de Sant Antoni 41; tapas from €4, sandwiches €8-11; ⏰6am-3am; 🍴; Ⓜ Sant Antoni)

Tickets

MODERN SPANISH €€€

14 Map p126, D1

This is, literally, one of the sizzling tickets in the restaurant world, a tapas bar opened by Ferran Adrià, of the legendary El Bulli, and his brother Albert.

And unlike El Bulli, it's an affordable venture – if you can book a table, that is. You can only book online, and two months in advance (or call for last-minute cancellations). (☎606 225545; www.ticketsbar.es; Avinguda del Paral·lel 164; tapas €5-27; ⏰6.30-10.30pm Tue-Fri, 1-3pm & 7-10.30pm Sat, closed Aug; Ⓜ Paral·lel)

Drinking

La Caseta del Migdia   BAR

15 Map p126, E5

The effort of getting to what is, for all intents and purposes, a simple *chiringuito* (makeshift cafe-bar) is worth it. Stare out to sea over a beer or coffee by day. As sunset approaches the atmosphere changes, as lounge music (from samba to funk) wafts out over the hillside. Drinks aside, you can also order barbecue, fired up on the outdoor grills. (☎617 956572; www.lacaseta.org; Mirador del Migdia; ⏰8pm-1am Wed-Fri, from noon Sat & Sun, weekends only in winter; 🚌150)

Bar Olimpia   BAR

16 Map p126, F1

This great little neighborhood bar is a little slice of Barcelona history. It was here (and on the surrounding block), where the popular Olimpia Theatre Circus once performed way back in the 1930s. Today, the vaguely retro bar draws a diverse crowd, who come for house-made vermouth, snacks (like quesadillas, cheese plates, tuna

Beer and tapas

tartare), and satisfying gin and tonics. (☎606 200800; Carrer d'Aldana 11; ⏰7pm-1am Wed & Thu, to 2.30am Fri & Sat, 6-11pm Sun; Ⓜ Paral·lel)

La Terrrazza   CLUB

17 Map p126, B3

One of the city's top summertime dance locations, La Terrrazza attracts squadrons of beautiful people, locals and foreigners alike, for a full-on night of music and cocktails partly under the stars inside the Poble Espanyol complex. (☎687 969825; www.laterrrazza.com; Avinguda de Francesc Ferrer i Guàrdia; €15-20; ⏰12.30am-6am Thu-Sat, closed Oct-Apr; Ⓜ Espanya)

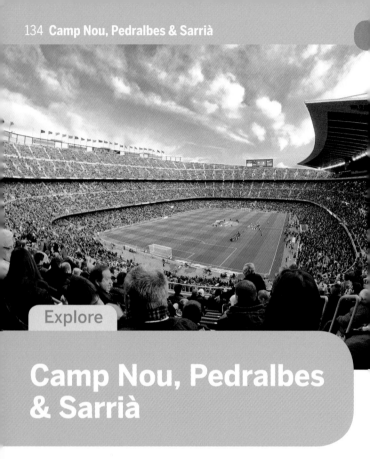

Explore

Camp Nou, Pedralbes & Sarrià

Camp Nou, home of FC Barcelona, is one of the greatest sporting temples on earth and a touchstone of Catalan identity. Up the hill to the north, village-like Sarrià belongs to a very different Barcelona. It's a refined, upmarket neighbourhood that bears little resemblance to the touristy downtown area. Leafy Pedralbes nearby is home to an enchanting medieval monastery.

The Sights in a Day

☀ Like most Barcelona attractions, **Camp Nou** (pictured left; p136) is a popular spot, so go early to beat the heavy crowds that arrive by midday. A longish walk uphill (or short cab ride) takes you to the small but splendidly landscaped **Jardins del Palau de Pedralbes** (p139). After some leafy exploration, continue to **Vivanda** (p140) for an outstanding lunch.

☀ After lunch, walk it off along the narrow lanes of Old Sarrià. Stop in for a chocolate fix at **Foix de Sarrià** (p140) and perhaps a drink or a snack of the famed *patatas bravas* at **Bar Tomàs** (p140). Stroll over (or take a taxi) to the atmospheric **Museu-Monestir de Pedralbes** (p139), where you can spend the rest of the afternoon exploring this well-preserved medieval monastery.

☾ The best way to end the night is at a lively FC Barcelona game at **Camp Nou** (p136), followed perhaps by celebratory drinks at **Lizarran** (p141). Afterwards, head over to lovely Plaça de la Concòrdia for a nightcap at **El Maravillas** (p141).

 Top Sights

Camp Nou & the Camp Nou Experience (p136)

♥ **Best of Barcelona**

Restaurants

Vivanda (p140)

Bangkok Cafe (p141)

Getting There

Ⓜ **Metro** Collblanc (line 5) and Les Corts (line 3) are the best stations for reaching Camp Nou.

🚃 **FGC** The easiest way to get to Sarrià (Sarrià and La Bonanova stations) and the Museu-Monestir de Pedralbes (Reina Elisenda) is by suburban train from Catalunya station in the city centre.

Top Sights
Camp Nou

FC Barcelona, the world's most successful football club, plays at Camp Nou, a stadium well matched with the grandeur of the team's achievements. Built in 1957 and enlarged for the 1992 World Cup, the stadium holds 99,000 people and is one of the world's largest. The stadium and club are also essential pillars in understanding how Catalans see themselves. To learn what all the fuss is about, come see a game or visit the Camp Nou Experience, a self-guided tour through the stadium and an interactive museum.

◉ Map p138, B4

www.fcbarcelona.com

Gate 9, Avinguda de Joan XXIII

adult/child €23/18

🕑 9.30am-7.30pm daily Apr-Sep, 10am-6.30pm Mon-Sat, to 2.30pm Sun Oct-Mar

Ⓜ Palau Reial

Don't Miss

A Real, Live Game

Tours of an empty stadium are one thing, but there's nothing like turning up to watch Barça strut their stuff live. Buying tickets is possible online, at FC Botiga shops and at tourist offices. You can also purchase at the Camp Nou ticket office (Gate 9).

Camp Nou Experience

On this self-guided tour, you'll get an in-depth look at the club, starting with a museum filled with multimedia exhibits, trophies and historical displays, followed by a tour of the stadium. It begins in FC Barcelona's museum, which has goal videos, trophies and displays on the club's history, its social commitment and connection to Catalan identity.

Behind the Scenes

The Camp Nou Experience tour takes in the visiting team's dressing room, heads out through the tunnel, and on to the edge of the pitch: standing where so many football greats once stood can be a powerful experience for FCB fans. You'll also get to visit the television studio, the press room and the commentary boxes. Set aside about 2½ hours for the whole visit.

FC Barcelona Megastore

Whether you're heading to a game or visiting the Camp Nou Experience, don't miss the sprawling three-storey FCB Megastore on the grounds of the stadium. You'll find all manner of goods emblazoned with Barça's famous scarlet and blue insignia. Via touchscreens, you can even order a customised shirt with your name and preferred number, that will be ready for you that same day.

☑ Top Tips

▶ To make the Camp Nou Experience tour, enter at Gate 9 (Avinguda de Joan XXIII near Carrer de Martí i Franquès).

▶ On game day, there are plenty of scalpers selling tickets; make sure you're safely seated before paying up.

▶ If you have a ticket for a game, go well before kick-off to soak up the atmosphere and to make sure you find your seat in this vast stadium.

✕ Take a Break

Just inside the gates (but outside the stadium itself), you'll find a few open-air eating and drinking spots, including a branch of Tapas 24.

You can also grab tapas and drinks at Lizarran (p141), located about a 15-minute walk from Camp Nou off Travessera de les Corts.

SARRIÀ

C de Ramon
Miquel i Planas

Reina Elisenda

Pg de la Reina Elisenda
de Montcada

Parc de
l'Oreneta

Museu-
Monéstir de
Pedralbes

C del Bisbe Català

Ronda de Dalt

Pg de la
Bonanova

Plaça
de Sarrià

C Major de Sarrià

C de Mañe
i Flaquer

C de
Rocaberti

Sarrià

C d'Angli

Via Augusta

C del Dr Roux

C de les Escoles Pies

C d'Iradier

Les Tres
Torres

Ronda del General Mitre

C de
Gandúxer

C de Copèrr

C de Freixa

C de Rase

La Bonanova

PEDRALBES

Av de Pedralbes

Pg dels Tillers

Parc
del Palau
Real

Pavellons Güell

Jardins del Palau
de Pedralbes

C de Jordi Girona

Palau Reial

C de Capità Arenas

Maria
Cristina

Plaça de la
Reina Maria
Cristina

C de Numància

Av Diagonal

C de Bori i Fontestà

Av de Sarr

C d'Ente

Plaç
de Sant Grego
Taumatu

C de
Déu i Mata

Jardins de
Sant Joan
de Déu

Parc
de les
Corts

C de Nicara

Av Diagonal

ZONA
UNIVERSITÀRIA

Av del Doctor Marañón

LES CORTS

Cementiri
de Les
Corts

Av de Joan XXIII

Camp
Nou

C d'Aristides Maillol

Travessera de
Les Corts

Jardins de
Bacardí

Av de Madrid

C d'Europa

Plaça de
les Comas

C de les Corts

Gran Via de Carles III

Les
Corts

C de Joan Güell

Jardins
de les
Infantes

Plaça del
Centre

C de Violant d'Hongria

C de Melcior de Palau

SANTS

C de Bert

Plaça
de Joa
Peiró

Badal

Collblanc

LA TORRASSA

C de Sants

Plaça de
Sants

N
0   400 r
0   0.2 miles

For reviews see	
◉ Top Sights	p136
◎ Sights	p139
✕ Eating	p140
☻ Drinking	p141

Sights

Museu-Monestir de Pedralbes

MONASTERY

1 ◉ Map p138, A2

This peaceful old convent was first opened to the public in 1983 and is now a museum of monastic life (the few remaining nuns have moved into more modern neighbouring buildings). It stands at the top of Avinguda de Pedralbes in a residential area that was countryside until the 20th century, and which remains a divinely quiet corner of Barcelona. (☏ 93 256 34 34; monestirpedralbes.bcn.cat; Baixada del Monestir 9; adult/child €5/free, 3-8pm Sun free; ⏱ 10am-5pm Tue-Fri, to 7pm Sat, to 8pm Sun; ☒ 22, 63, 64, 75, ☒ FGC Reina Elisenda)

Jardins del Palau de Pedralbes

PARK

2 ◉ Map p138, B3

A few steps from busy Avinguda Diagonal lies this small enchanting green space. Sculptures, fountains, citrus trees, bamboo groves, fragrant eucalyptus, towering cypresses and bougainvillea-covered nooks lie scattered along the paths criss-crossing these peaceful gardens. Among the little-known treasures here are a vine-covered parabolic pergola and a gurgling fountain of Hercules, both designed by Antoni Gaudí. (Avinguda Diagonal 686; ⏱ 10am-8pm Apr-Oct, to 6pm Nov-Mar; Ⓜ Palau Reial)

 Local Life

A Wander Through Old Sarrià

Just west of Via Augusta, the old centre of Sarrià is a largely pedestrianised haven of peace. Probably founded in the 13th century and only incorporated into Barcelona in 1921, ancient Sarrià is formed around sinuous Carrer Major de Sarrià – today a mix of old and new, with a sprinkling of shops and restaurants. At its top end is pretty **Plaça de Sarrià**. As you wander downhill, duck off into Plaça del Consell de la Vila, Plaça de Sant Vicenç de Sarrià and Carrer de Rocaberti, at the end of which is the **Monestir de Santa Isabel** with its neo-Gothic cloister.

Pavellons Güell

ARCHITECTURE

3 ◉ Map p138, B3

A short stroll from the Jardins del Palau de Pedralbes are the stables and porter's lodge designed by Gaudí for the Finca Güell, as the Güell estate here was called. The structures here were built in the mid-1880s, when Gaudí was strongly impressed by Islamic architecture. You can peer inside on guided visits, with English-language tours at 10.15am, 11.15pm and 3pm. Unexpected closures can occur, so it's wise to confirm opening hours before heading out.

One of the most eye-catching features here is the fantastic wrought-iron dragon gate near Avinguda de

Pedralbes. (📞93 317 76 52; Avinguda de Pedralbes 7; guided tours adult/child €4/2; 🕙10am-4pm; Ⓜ Palau Reial)

Eating

Foix de Sarrià   PASTELERÍA €

4 🍽 Map p138, B1

Since 1886 this exclusive pastry shop has been selling the most exquisite cakes and sweets. You can take them away or head out the back to sip tea, coffee or hot chocolate while sampling the little cakes and other wizardry. (📞93 203 04 73; www.foixdesarria.com; Plaça de Sarrià 12-13; desserts €2-5; 🕗8am-9pm; 🚆FGC Reina Elisenda)

Bar Tomàs   TAPAS €

5 🍽 Map p138, B2

Many *barcelonins* have long claimed that Bar Tomàs is by far the best place in the city for *patatas bravas* (potato chunks in a slightly spicy tomato sauce). Despite the fluorescent lights and friendly but gruff service, folks from all walks of life pile in, particularly for lunch on weekends. (📞93 203 10 77; Carrer Major de Sarrià 49; tapas €2.50-5.50; 🕙noon-4pm & 6-10pm Mon-Sat; 🚆FGC Sarrià)

Santamasa   CATALAN €

6 🍽 Map p138, B1

Next door to Sarrià's pretty 18th-century church (Sant Vicenç de Sarrià), Santamassa is an enticing spot for a light meal at any time of day. The menu here is wide-ranging, with a mix of creatively topped *pizzetes* (small pizzas), salads, open-faced sandwiches, fondue, burgers, quesadillas and good sharing appetisers like hummus and guacamole. (📞93 676 35 74; Carrer Major de Sarrià 97; mains €7-12; 🕘9am-midnight; 🚆FGC Reina Elisenda)

Vivanda   CATALAN €€

7 🍽 Map p138, B1

With a menu designed by celebrated Catalan chef Jordi Vilà, diners are in for a treat at this Sarrià classic. The changing dishes showcase seasonal fare (like eggs with truffles, rice with cuttlefish, and artichokes with romesco sauce).One of Vivanda's best features is the garden-like terrace hidden behind the restaurant. With heat lamps, it's open year-round – blankets and hot broth are distributed to diners in winter. (📞93 203 19 18; www.vivanda.cat; Carrer Major de Sarrià 134; sharing plates €8-18; 🕜1.30-3.30pm Tue-Sun & 9-11pm Tue-Sat; 🚆FGC Reina Elisenda)

5° Pino   CATALAN €€

8 🍽 Map p138, B1

While exploring Sarrià, it's worth detouring a few blocks east to this charming cafe and restaurant, which is a favourite local spot for tasty sandwiches, salads, tortillas, tapas and drinks. It's on a busy road, though the outdoor, pine-shaded terrace is still a pleasant spot for a bite.

The adjoining playground (best for kids under six) adds to the appeal for

Wine and tapas

PAMELA R/SHUTTERSTOCK ©

most Catalan eateries. (☎93 339 32 69; Carrer d'Evarist Arnús 65; mains €10-13; ◷7.45-11pm Tue-Sun & 1-3.30pm Fri-Sun; MPlaça del Centre)

Drinking

El Maravillas
COCKTAIL BAR

10 📍 Map p138, D3

Overlooking the peaceful Plaça de la Concòrdia, El Maravillas feels like a secret hideaway – especially if you've just arrived from the crowded lanes of the *ciutat vella* (old city). The glittering bar has just a few tables, with outdoor seating on the square when the weather warms. Creative cocktails, good Spanish red wines and easy-drinking vermouths are the drinks of choice. (☎93 360 73 78; Plaça de la Concòrdia 15; ◷noon-midnight Mon-Thu, to 2am Fri & Sat; MMaria Cristina)

Lizarran
BAR

11 📍 Map p138, C4

This is a fine pre- or postgame drinking spot if you're catching an FC Barcelona game at Camp Nou. The beer is plentiful and cheap, there's a decent tapas selection, and on warm days you can sit on the pleasant terrace at the front. From here it's about a 15-minute walk to the stadium. (Carrer de Can Bruixa 6; ◷8am-midnight Sun-Thu, to 2am Fri & Sat; MLes Corts)

parents with little ones in tow. (Quinto Pino; ☎93 252 22 81; www.quintopino.es; Passeig de la Bonanova 98; sandwiches €9-13, tapas €4-8; ◷8.30am-1.30am Mon-Fri, 10am-1.30am Sat & Sun; 🚉FGC Sarrià)

Bangkok Cafe
THAI €€

9 🍴 Map p138, D4

If you're craving Thai cuisine, it's well worth making the trip out to Bangkok Cafe, which serves up spicy green papaya salad, *tam yam kung* (spicy prawn soup), crispy prawns with plum sauce, red curries and other standouts, with more spice than you'll find in

The Best of
Barcelona

Bar Pastis (p54), El Raval
FERNANDO VAZQUEZ MIRAS/GETTY IMAGES ©

Best Walks
The Old City in a Day

🏃 The Walk

The triptych of the Barri Gòtic, La Ribera and El Raval is where Barcelona was born. The Barri Gòtic is the old city's heart and soul, while El Raval is a vibrant mix of vintage storefronts and immigrant arrivistes. La Ribera, with El Born, is quintessential Barcelona – an icon of cool, but home to attractions of more enduring legacy. This walk takes you through these areas, past fabulous museums, monuments to antiquity, intimate squares and along the irresistible La Rambla.

Start Museu Picasso; Ⓜ Jaume I

Finish MACBA; Ⓜ Universitat

Length 2.5km; two hours

🍴 Take a Break

Art deco and bohemian, **Cafè de L'Òpera** (p25) has had a front-row seat on La Rambla since 1929 and is the perfect old-city rest stop.

ANSNAR/SHUTTERSTOCK©

La Catedral (p28)

❶ Museu Picasso

The **Museu Picasso** (p58) is best visited early in the morning, making it the ideal place to begin your walk. Apart from the early Picasso paintings that so distinguish this museum, the medieval mansions that make up the gallery have been beautifully preserved.

❷ Basílica de Santa Maria del Mar

Carrer de Montcada, a typical old-city lane – narrow, boisterous and leading somewhere interesting – passes some fine tapas bars, then emerges at the lovely, shaded Passeig del Born (on your left) with the **Basílica de Santa Maria del Mar** (p62) on your right. A pinnacle of Catalan Gothic, this church is all grace, light and elegance within.

❸ La Catedral

Out the church's southwest door, Plaça de Santa Maria del Mar is a lovely little square, from which pedestrianised Carrer de l'Argenteria leads northwest to the Barri Gòtic. Pass the remnants of Roman walls, and continue onto the Gothic centrepiece of Barcelona's oldest quarter, **La Catedral** (p28), which is at once both sombre and a gilded study in excess.

④ Plaça de Sant Josep Oriol

Plaça de Sant Josep Oriol is one of the most charming squares of the Barri Gòtic. **Església de Santa Maria del Pi** (p34) looms overhead, while old shops and bars front the plaza.

Outdoor tables make a fine setting for a bite or a drink.

⑤ Plaça Reial

More lanes lead through the heart of the old city to the grandest of old Barcelona's squares, **Plaça Reial** (p34), which is ringed by bars and eateries. Don't miss the wild lamp posts of early Gaudí vintage.

⑥ La Rambla

Cutting through old Barcelona, **La Rambla** (p24) transports a

river of people from L'Eixample to the sea. Walk northwest through this tide of people and performers before launching off its western shore into El Raval.

⑦ MACBA

Cutting-edge galleries are a speciality in Barcelona, and the **MACBA** (p51) is one of the finest. Fusing a modern collection, stunning contemporary architecture and the shell of an ancient monastery, this place is Barcelona in one integrated whole.

Best Walks
Modernista Barcelona

🏃 The Walk

The Modernista architecture personified by (but not restricted to) Antoni Gaudí is Barcelona's most eye-catching signature. Examples ripple out across the city, but L'Eixample has the greatest concentration. With undulating facades, otherworldly interiors, imaginative rooftops and nary a straight line in sight, Modernista L'Eixample is unlike any other urban landscape on earth. This itinerary showcases why many visitors can't get enough of this breathtaking city.

Start Plaça de Catalunya; Ⓜ Catalunya

Finish La Sagrada Família; Ⓜ Sagrada Família

Length 3km; three hours

✖ Take a Break

Barcelona's tapas chefs are to contemporary cuisine what Gaudí was to early 20th-century architecture. This is exemplified at much-celebrated **Tapas 24** (p101).

Casa de les Punxes

❶ Casa Amatller

If Barcelona has a Champs-Élysées equivalent, it's Passeig de Gràcia, and close to its midpoint are some extraordinary Modernista delights. **Casa Amatller** (p98), a masterpiece by Josep Puig i Cadafalch with echoes of gabled northern Europe, is one of the standouts.

❷ Casa Batlló

You know you've arrived at **Casa Batlló** (p92) when you stumble upon dozens of passers-by gazing up at the facade with a mix of awe and amusement. Most visitors have the same reaction inside, where Gaudí turns the conception of interior space on its head.

❸ Fundació Antoni Tàpies

Designed by Domènech i Montaner, the **Fundació Antoni Tàpies** (p99) is a brick and iron building with both Islamic-inspired details and elements of pure whimsy. Note the vibrant chaos swirling over the roof, imagined by the late Antonio

Tàpies himself, whose staggering collection of paintings lies within.

④ La Pedrera

A little further up the hill along Passeig de Gràcia, **La Pedrera** (p90) is similarly adorned with a fine facade in the best Gaudí tradition, but it's the interior (the attic is like inhabiting a fossil, the apartment like inhabiting a dream) and the rooftop that transform this apartment building into the realm of genius.

⑤ Palau del Baró Quadras

The Modernistas were inspired by everything from Gothic to Orientalist styles and you'll find all of these on show in the **Palau del Baró Quadras** (p99). It's the work of Puig i Cadafalch, a towering Modernista genius.

⑥ Casa de les Punxes

Nowhere does the Modernista aesthetic intersect so clearly with the childlike evocation of a fairy tale than in Puig i Cadafalch's Casa de les Punxes. Turrets resemble witches' hats in this castle-like flight of neo-Gothic fancy.

⑦ La Sagrada Família

Nothing compares to **La Sagrada Família** (p108). Gaudí's unfinished masterwork is quite simply one of the world's foremost architectural creations, at once the high point of the Modernista style and a work so utterly original as to deserve a category of its own.

Best Walks
Food Lover's Barcelona

🏃 The Walk

Barcelona is synonymous with food of the highest quality and the ways to sample this are seemingly endless, from ageless tapas bars and Michelin-starred restaurants to roiling markets and corner shops that have been selling the finest local products for more than a century. Food in this city is a way of life and one of the more pleasurable ways to enter into the local culture. This walk begins that process of initiation.

Start Quimet i Quimet; M Paral·lel

Finish Comerç 24; M Arc de Triomf

Length 3.5km; three to four hours

🍴 Take a Break

In a medieval-like setting in the Barri Gòtic, the **Cafè de l'Acadèmia** (p36) serves outstanding Catalan fare, and you can dine out on the plaza on warm sunny days.

Mercat de la Boqueria (p46)

❶ Quimet i Quimet

Choosing our favourite tapas bar in a city that's world-famous for them is no easy task, but **Quimet i Quimet** (p132) would always make the shortlist. Catalan tapas par excellence, bottles of every alcoholic beverage imaginable and an agreeable atmosphere built up over five generations are a near-perfect recipe.

❷ Granja M Viader

Barcelona's tradition of milk bars finds its most famous expression in the timeless **Granja M Viader** (p49) in El Raval. Its milk-chocolate drinks are renowned and the ambience is a cross between American diner and 19th-century Barcelona.

❸ Mercat de la Boqueria

Barcelona's best market, the **Mercat de la Boqueria** (p46), is the most easily accessible of all Barcelona's culinary traditions. It's here that the city's celebrated chefs do their shopping, and it's all about colour, quality and people who take their food seriously.

❹ Caelum

One peculiarity of Spanish cuisine is the food that emerges from convents all across the country. Many of these items have been packaged up, along with other rare and artisan-made delicacies, and offered for sale at **Caelum** (p40). Stay long enough for a coffee in the medieval basement.

❺ Formatgeria La Seu

Dedicated to artisan cheeses from all across Spain, the tiny Formatgeria La Seu is the antithesis of mass production – it sells only the best from small-scale farmers and the stock changes regularly. Wine and cheese tastings in the cosy room at the back are fun.

❻ Hofmann Pastisseria

No matter the time of day, it's never the wrong moment to bite into a plump raspberry-filled croissant, crispy hazelnut cookie or a decadent cake, provided they come from **Hofmann Pastisseria** (p74). Get a few treats

to go, and devour them on Passeig del Born.

❼ Bormuth

Bormuth (p70) has tapped into the vogue for old-school tapas with modern-times service and decor, and serves all the old favourites – *patatas bravas, ensaladilla* (Russian salad), tortilla – along with some less predictable and superbly prepared numbers (try the chargrilled red pepper with black pudding).

Best
Restaurants

Barcelona is one of Europe's richest culinary capitals and there are few corners of the city where you can't find highly regarded cuisine. Traditional Catalan is the mainstay, but there are also ultramodern designer temples to gastronomic experimentation and places serving dishes from the rest of Spain.

LOOK DIE BILDAGENTUR DER FOTOGRAFEN GMBH/ALAMY STOCK PHOTO ©

New Wave Catalan

Avant-garde chefs have made Catalonia famous throughout the world for their food laboratories, their commitment to food as art and their crazy riffs on the themes of traditional local cooking. Here the notion of gourmet cuisine is deconstructed as chefs transform liquids into foams, create 'ice cream' of classic ingredients, freeze-dry foods to make concentrated powder versions and employ spherification to produce artful concoctions.

Traditional Catalan

Traditional Catalan recipes showcase the great produce of the Mediterranean: fish, prawns, cuttlefish, clams, pork, rabbit, game, olive oil and loads of garlic. Classic dishes also feature unusual pairings such as cuttlefish with chickpeas, cured pork with caviar, rabbit with prawns or goose with pears.

Seafood

There is a wealth of restaurants specialising in seafood. Not surprisingly, Barceloneta, which lies near the sea, is packed with eateries of all shapes and sizes doling out decadent paellas and deliciously grilled catch of the day. A few classic dishes to look out for include *arròs a la marinera* (seafood rice), *fideuà* (a vermicelli noodle variant of paella), *suquet* (fish stew) and *bollabessa de peix i marisc* (fish and seafood bouillabaisse).

Best Traditional Catalan

Cafè de l'Acadèmia Superb Catalan gastronomy in an enchanting Barri Gòtic setting. (p36)

Suculent High-quality traditional recipes from culinary superstar Carles Abellán. (p53)

Mam i Teca Catalan cooking done right in El Raval. (p52)

Casa Calvet A memorable feast dining in a Gaudí building. (pictured above; p104)

Vivanda Magnificent Catalan cooking with year-round dining in the garden. (p140)

La Vinateria del Call Romantic medieval setting for decadent traditional recipes. (p35)

Can Culleretes The city's oldest restaurant, with great-value traditional dishes. (p31)

Best Seafood

Passadís del Pep Well-kept local secret for the freshest seafood in Barcelona. (p70)

La Cova Fumada Bustling down-at-the-heels eatery serving magnificent sea-centric small plates in Barceloneta. (p79)

Barraca Mouth-watering paellas and rice dishes at this seafront favourite. (p86)

Can Maño Humble looking tavern that serves excellent seafood at affordable prices. (p86)

Best New Wave

Disfrutar A new and avant-garde addition that has rapidly become Barcelona's most talked-about restaurant. (p104)

Cinc Sentits Michelin-starred and a laboratory for creative cookery. (p104)

Pla Old-style setting, new-style taste combinations with discernible roots in local traditions. (p38)

Tickets The celebrated restaurant of Albert Adrià, showcasing Barcelona's best *nueva cocina española*. (p132)

Best Vegetarian

Flax & Kale Delectable, colourful salads and a truly creative approach. (p52)

Rasoterra Creative vegetarian dishes with a wide range of European and Eastern influences. (p36)

Amaltea A much-loved meat-free eatery in L'Eixample. (p101)

Best International

Koy Shunka Dine at the wraparound counter and watch the master sushi chefs prepare morsels of perfection. (p38)

El Atril Aussie-influenced menu (including kangaroo fillet) and outdoor dining. (p70)

Bangkok Cafe Hands down Barcelona's best Southeast Asian cooking. (p141)

Casa Delfín Delicious Mediterranean fare served in an atmospheric setting. (p71)

Best Desserts

Foix De Sarrià Selling delicate and delightful cakes and sweets since 1886. (p140)

Caelum Dine on sweet perfection in the pleasant cafe, or head downstairs for medieval atmosphere. (p40)

Worth a Trip

Northwest of Barceloneta in Poblenou, **Can Recasens** (☎93 300 81 23; Rambla del Poblenou 102; mains €7-15; ⏰9pm-1am Mon-Sat & 1-4pm Sat; Ⓜ Poblenou) hides a warren of warmly lit rooms full of oil paintings and fairy lights. The food is outstanding, with a mix of salads, fondues, smoked meats, cheeses and open-faced sandwiches piled high with delicacies like wild mushrooms and brie or *escalivada* (grilled vegetables) and Gruyère.

Best
Tapas

Tapas, those bite-sized morsels of genius, are an essential pillar in Barcelona's culinary culture. Like all elements of Catalan cuisine, the breadth of choice when it comes to tapas is extraordinary, from the traditional Catalan way of serving seafood from a can to astonishing little taste combinations whose origins lie in a laboratory.

LUCIA LAMBRIEX/GETTY IMAGES ©

Tapas Bars

As per the 'bar' designation, these places are less formal than restaurants, and drinking is an essential component in the experience. Indeed tapas eating often happens on bar stools, or sometimes standing around at counters. Given much of the food is ready to eat when you arrive, the tapas bar makes a good option if you want something in a hurry, or hit a few tapas spots on a bar crawl around town.

How to Tapas

Ordering tapas generally works like this: you take your seat at the bar or one of the cafe-style tables usually on hand, order drinks – try the *txacolí* (slightly fizzy white wine), a glass of *cava* (sparkling wine), a house-made *vermut* (vermouth) or a refreshing *caña* (draught beer) – and ask for a plate. Some places merely have plates stacked up, and you help yourself. Many of the tapas are *montaditos* (presented on a slice of bread), which can range from a creamy Roquefort-cheese-and-walnut combination to a chunk of spicy sausage. They all come with toothpicks. These facilitate their consumption, but serve another important purpose, too: when you're ready to leave, the toothpicks are counted up and the bill presented.

☑ **Top Tips**

▶ Tapas is best enjoyed as a predinner snack; trying to make a full meal out of it can prove expensive.

▶ While a tapa is a tiny serving, if you particularly like something you can have a *ración* (full plate-size serving) or *media ración* (half plate-size serving).

Pintxos

Best Traditional Tapas

Quimet i Quimet Award-winning morsels, top wine choices beer, and fifth-generation hospitality. (p132)

La Cova Fumada Always packed, this down-at-the-heels spot deserves its neighbourhood fame. (p79)

Bar Pinotxo Pull up a bar stool at this legendary tapas joint in the Mercat de la Boqueria. (p47)

El Xampanyet Swirls of anchovies and a timeless atmosphere. (p65)

Elisabets Unchanged in decades and good for Catalan *fuet* (sausage) or filled rolls. (p49)

Bar Ramón Delicious small plates in an old-school, rock-loving setting. (p125)

Cal Pep Traditional with the occasional twist at this long-standing tapas haunt. (p65)

Vaso de Oro Grilled prawns as they should be, in Barceloneta. (p79)

Bar Tomàs Down-and-dirty bar with peerless *patatas bravas* (potato chunks in a slightly spicy tomato sauce). (p140)

Best Designer Tapas

Tickets The celebrated eatery from molecular gastronomy star Albert Adrià. (p132)

Tapas 24 Riffs on traditional tapas varieties in a slick white L'Eixample basement. (p101)

Cata 1.81 The whole world is an inspiration for the tapas here. (p102)

Palo Cortao A new star in Poble Sec with outstanding sharing plates. (p132)

Bormuth Serves a delightful mix of the classic and the new wave, plus refreshing vermouths. (p70)

Kaiku Handsome Barceloneta eatery with deliciously creative dishes. (p84)

Belmonte Innovative Catalan dishes are served in a cosy Barri Gòtic setting. (p36)

Best Regional Tapas

Euskal Etxea Basque *pintxos* lined up along the bar three storeys high in El Born. (p65)

Bar del Pla Tapas from all over Spain take on new life and direction. (p65)

Best
Shopping

A world-class shopping destination, Barcelona has a sense of style that pervades everything from fashion and home accessories to food shops, markets, antiques and handicrafts. Fashion's true home is L'Eixample and the streets surrounding the iconic Passeig de Gràcia. Elsewhere, boutiques in narrow old-city lanes make you feel like you've stumbled upon hidden treasure.

IAN AITKEN/GETTY IMAGES ©

Fashion

You'll find boutiques devoted to the big Spanish designers alongside respected Catalan designers, such as the enduring Armand Basi and the celebrated and youthful Custo Dalmau. And there's barely an international brand that doesn't have an outlet in Barcelona. The grid-like streets in the heart of L'Eixample – known as the Quadrat d'Or (Golden Square) – offer the richest pickings.

Food & Drink

Produce markets may grab the attention – the Mercat de la Boqueria could be Europe's finest – but Barcelona is also studded with little gourmet food stores, some unchanged in a century, others riding some new wave as is the Barcelona way. They're the perfect places to shop for a picnic or souvenirs.

Antiques & Homewares

Barcelona's old city – the Barri Gòtic, La Ribera and El Raval – is a splendid place to set off on a treasure hunt, because it's in these twisting lanes that traditions survive, whether in the form of antiques, quirky local crafts or retro furnishings. High-end design shops are best found in L'Eixample where you can find cutting-edge designer homewares in every imaginable form.

Best Stores

La Manual Alpargatera Famed, old-fashioned shop in the Barri Gòtic specialising in espadrilles (rope-soled canvas shoes). (p43)

Amapola Vegan Shop Handsome shoes, bags and accessories all made from animal-free products. (p113)

Regia A legendary L'Eixample perfume shop, in business since the 1920s. (p106)

Magnesia A jewel box of a store in Gràcia with great gift ideas. (p113)

Loisaida Men and women's fashion, antiques and retro vinyl. (p75)

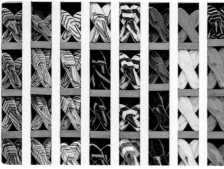

Colourful espadrilles for sale

Lurdes Bergada Top-notch fashion boutique with high-quality apparel for men and women. (p94)

Bagués-Masriera Where else could you find jewellery crafted into Modernista forms? (p95)

Best Food & Drink Shops

Mercat de la Boqueria Fresh food market and mother lode of Barcelona's culinary culture. (p46)

Caelum Sweets, preserves and convent-cooked cookies from all over Spain. (p40)

Casa Gispert Roast nuts of every type, plus chocolate, conserves and olive oils. (p74)

Foix de Sarrià Artfully made cakes and pastries that look almost too good to eat. (p140)

Joan Múrria The finest edible products from Catalonia and elsewhere in Spain. (p107)

Best Antiques & Homewares

Port Antic Market A small but lively weekend antiques market near the end of La Rambla. (p87)

El Bulevard dels Antiquaris A labyrinth of tiny antique shops that merits a morning's browsing. (p106)

Worth a Trip

Barcelona's most authentic flea market, **Els Encants Vells** (Fira de Bellcaire; 93 246 30 30; www.encantsbcn.com; Plaça de les Glòries Catalanes; 9am-8pm Mon, Wed, Fri & Sat; M Glòries), northeast of L'Eixample, is where bargain-hunters rifle through everything from battered old shoes and bric-a-brac to antique furniture and new clothes. Go in the morning for the best choice.

Best
Architecture

Few cities are defined by their architecture to quite the same extent as Barcelona. The weird and wonderful undulations of Antoni Gaudí's creations are echoed in countless Modernista flights of fancy across the city. But Barcelona's architecture is a multidimensional story, which begins with Gothic grandeur and continues with a spirit of contemporary innovation that adds depth to this remarkable cityscape.

Gothic Barcelona

Barcelona is one of Europe's Gothic treasure chests, and it was largely from these jewels that the Modernistas took their inspiration. Catalan Gothic took its own course, with decoration used sparingly and Catalan builders championing breadth over height.

The Modernistas

Modernisme emerged in Barcelona during the 1880s, the city's belle époque. While the name suggests a rejection of the old, pioneers of the style actually delved deep into the past for inspiration, absorbed everything they could and then ripped up the rulebook. For many, Modernisme is synonymous with Gaudí (1852–1926), but he was by no means alone. Lluís Domènech i Montaner (1850–1923) and Josep Puig i Cadafalch (1867–1957) left a wealth of remarkable buildings across the city.

Contemporary Architecture

Barcelona's unrelenting openness to new ideas and the latest trends in art and design ensure local and international architects find fertile ground for adding daring new elements to the city's skyline.

ALIONABIRUKOVA/GETTY IMAGES ©

Best Gothic Giants

La Catedral The old city's Gothic centrepiece, at once extravagant and sombre. (p28)

Basílica de Santa Maria del Mar Arguably the high point of Catalan Gothic. (p62)

Església de Santa Maria del Pi A 14th-century jewel with a dazzling rose window. (p34)

Museu Marítim In the former Gothic shipyards just off the seaward end of La Rambla. (pictured above; p82)

Museu-Monestir de Pedralbes A 14th-century monastery with a superb three-level cloister. (p139)

Museu Picasso Rare surviving examples of Gothic mansions, now converted artfully into exhibition space. (p58)

Fundació Antoni Tàpies

Best of Gaudí

La Sagrada Família
Gaudí's unfinished
symphony. (p108)

La Pedrera Showpiece
Gaudí apartment building
with an otherworldly roof.
(p90)

Casa Batlló An eye-
catching facade, with an
astonishing interior to
match. (p92)

Palau Güell Gaudí's only
building in the old part of
town. (p51)

Park Güell Gaudí's
playfulness in full swing.
(p114)

Best of the Modernista Rest

**Palau de la Música
Catalana** Breathtak-
ing concert hall by Lluís
Domènech i Montaner.
(p68)

Casa Amatller Josep
Puig i Cadafalch's neigh-
bour to Casa Batlló with
gabled roof. (p98)

Casa Lleó Morera
Ornate facade of dancing
nymphs, rooftop cupolas
and interior stained glass.
(p98)

Fundació Antoni Tàpies
A brick and iron-framed
masterpiece designed by
Domènech i Montaner.
(p99)

**Recinte Modernista de
Sant Pau** Gilded pavil-
ions north of La Sagrada
Família by Domènech i
Montaner. (p98)

Palau del Baró Quadras
Stained-glass and neo-
Gothic flourishes by Puig
i Cadafalch. (p99)

Worth a Trip

A Gaudí mas-
terpiece recently
rescued from ob-
scurity, **Bellesguard**
(☏ 93 250 40 93; www.
bellesguardgaudi.com;
Carrer de Bellesguard 16;
€9; ⏱ 10am-3pm Tue-
Sun; 🚇 FGC Avinguda
Tibidabo) has a castle-
like appearance
that combines both
Gothic and Mod-
ernista elements.
Guided tours in
English happen on
weekends at 11am.
At other times, you
can wander the
interior and the
grounds with an
audioguide.

Best
Art & Design

Barcelona has for centuries been a canvas for great Spanish and Catalan artists – its streets, squares, parks and galleries are littered with the signatures of artists past and present. From Modernista sculptors, such as Josep Llimona, to international and home-grown stars, such as Roy Lichtenstein and Joan Miró, they've all left their mark.

AXIOM PHOTOGRAPHIC/GETTY IMAGES ©

Street Art

Since the return of democracy in the late 1970s, the town hall has not been shy about encouraging the placement of sometimes grandiose and often incomprehensible contemporary works in the city's public spaces. Among the works *barcelonins* regularly encounter: Frank Gehry's fish sculpture, which they walk beneath en route to Port Olímpic; a Joan Miró mosaic on La Rambla; and a rather baffling Antoni Tàpies sculpture on the edge of Parc de la Ciutadella (pictured above). There's even a soaring sculpture of intertwined wires, which pays homage to *castellers* (human castles), near city hall in Plaça de Sant Miquel.

Twentieth-Century Art

Two great names in 20th-century art – Pablo Picasso and Joan Miró – had strong ties to Barcelona, and both left considerable legacies in the city. Pivotal artwork from Picasso's early days is on show here, as is the most complete collection of Joan Miró's masterworks. Aside from these international figures, Barcelona has been a minor cauldron of activity, dominated by figures such as Antoni Tàpies. Early in his career (from the mid-1940s onwards) he seemed keen on self-portraits, but also experimented with collage using materials from wood to rice.

Best 20th-Century Art & Design

Museu Picasso A journey through Picasso's work before cubism took over his life. (p58)

Fundació Joan Miró Joan Miró's portfolio, from his formative years to later works. (p122)

Fundació Antoni Tàpies A selection of Tàpies' works and contemporary art exhibitions. (p99)

Museu Nacional d'Art de Catalunya Modern Catalan art on the upstairs floor of Barcelona's premier art museum. (p118)

MACBA Fabulous rotating collection of local and international contemporary art. (pictured above p51)

Gaudí-designed lamp post, Plaça Reial (p34)

Fundació Suñol Rich private collection of photography, sculpture and paintings (some by Picasso). (p100)

Centre de Cultura Contemporània de Barcelona High-class rotating exhibitions, often focusing on photography. (p51)

CaixaForum Dynamic artistic space in a beautifully converted Modernista building. (p128)

Museu del Modernisme Barcelona Modernistas (including Gaudí) turn their attention to home furnishings. (p100)

Best Street Art

Homenatge a la Barceloneta Rebecca Horn's tribute to Barceloneta's pre-Olympics waterfront culture. (p84)

Mosaïc de Miró The work of Barcelona's artistic icon adorns the footpath of La Rambla. (p26)

Gaudí's Lamp Posts One of Gaudí's earliest commissions in the Barri Gòtic's Plaça Reial. (p34)

Worth a Trip

Nicknamed *la grapadora* (the stapler) by locals, the rather brutalist **Museu del Disseny de Barcelona** (93 256 68 00; www.museudeldisseny.cat; Plaça de les Glòries Catalanes 37; permanent/temporary exhibition €6/4.40, combination ticket €8; 10am-8pm Tue-Sun; M Glòries) has a fascinating collection of exhibitions covering fashion, ceramics, textiles, graphic art and industrial design.

Best
Parks & Beaches

The tight tangle of lanes that constitutes Barcelona's old town can feel claustrophobic at times. But once you move beyond, Barcelona opens up as a city of light and space – its parks, gardens and long stretches of sand bequeathing the city an unmistakably Mediterranean air. Locals love nothing better than to immerse themselves in these open areas.

Scenic Parks & Gardens

The patchwork of parks and gardens that encircle central Barcelona to the east, west and north are much-loved focal points for local life – the ideal settings for picnics and the place to stroll, free from traffic and mass tourism. Parc de la Ciutadella and Park Güell are perhaps the best-known stands of green, but Montjuïc, on the steep rise that overlooks Barcelona from the west, offers the greatest variety for those looking to escape the noise of city life.

Beach Culture

Barcelona's love affair with the sea began in earnest in 1992, when the development accompanying the Olympics transformed its waterfront into a sophisticated promenade. Thankfully, not all of what went before was lost and Barceloneta retains elements of its one-time knockabout personality. It's a neighbourhood that combines those Mediterranean ideals of wonderful seafood, agreeable surrounds and a beach always close at hand. Yes, there are more beautiful beaches further along the coast, but Barcelona's city beaches are transformed by one simple fact: most lie within walking (or metro) distance of a city the world has come to love.

☑ Top Tips

▶ Shop for your picnic at Mercat de Santa Caterina (p68) en route to Parc de la Ciutadella.

▶ Ditto at Mercat de la Boqueria (p46) on the way to the gardens of Montjuïc.

▶ Eating options are sparse inside Park Güell – bring your own food here, too.

MARK MAWSON/ROBERTHARDING/GETTY IMAGES ©

Platja de Nova Icària

Best Parks & Gardens

Park Güell Everybody's favourite public park, where zany Gaudí flourishes meet landscape gardening. (p114)

Parc de la Ciutadella Home to parliament, a zoo, public art and abundant shade. (p68)

Jardins de Mossèn Cinto de Verdaguer Gentle, sloping Montjuïc gardens devoted to bulbs and water lilies. (p130)

Jardí Botànic More than 40,000 plants faithful to a loosely defined Mediterranean theme. (p130)

Jardins de Mossèn Costa i Llobera An exotic stand of tropical and desert flora. (p130)

Jardins del Mirador Good views and a handful of snack bars below the castle. (p130)

Best Beaches

Platja de Nova Icària Perhaps the loveliest of Barcelona's city beaches, located just beyond Port Olímpic.

Platja de la Barceloneta Plenty of sand and more of a locals' beach than others. (p78)

Platja de Sant Sebastià Family-friendly beach where Barceloneta meets the sea. (p78)

Worth a Trip

The five **beaches** stretching northeast from Port Olímpic (starting with **Platja de Nova Icària**, followed by **Platja de Bogatell**) have nicer sand and cleaner water. All have at least one *chiringuito* – snacks and drinks bars that are often open until 1am (late April to October).

Best
Sports &
Activities

RICHARD CUMMINS/GETTY IMAGES ©

The Mediterranean oceanfront and rambling hilly park overlooking the city make fine settings for a bit of outdoor activity beneath the (generally) sunny skies of Barcelona. For a break from museum-hopping and overindulging at tapas bars, Barcelona has the antidote – running, swimming, cycling or simply pumping fists in the air at a never-dull FC Barcelona match.

Running & Cycling

Barcelona's long enticing seafront makes a picturesque setting for a jog or a spin, with a bike lane separate from traffic and pedestrians. Montjuïc with its fine views is another good spot for exercise. The best time to go is early morning before the crowds (and heat) arrive.

Swimming & Surfing

If you like swimming in the sea, head to the beaches north of Platja de Nova Icària, which are cleaner than those nearer the port. Barcelona also has some great lap-swimming options, including several water-front sports centres near Barceloneta. You can also surf waves off the beaches (best from October to April) or go stand-up paddleboarding year-round, with beachside rentals hiring out equipment and wetsuits.

Spas & Relaxation

A day at the spa can be a fantastic way to recharge after a few days of exploring, or perhaps a few nights on the town. The best spas come replete with candlelit anterooms and sumptuous baths and steam rooms. Most high-end hotels have spas, though the more charming options are scattered around town.

FC Barcelona match Watch Messi and company take on the world in a live game. (p136)

Piscines Bernat Picornell Swim laps at Barcelona's official Olympic pool. (p129)

Port Olímpic Follow the waterfront to the former Olympic port, now a yacht marina. (pictured above; p79)

Molokai SUP Center Go for a stand-up paddleboarding adventure off Barceloneta. (p83)

Aire de Barcelona A beautiful Banys Àrabs–style spa in a historic setting in El Born. (p74)

Best
Views

LENA_SERDITOVA/GETTY IMAGES ©

Barcelona's position between sea and mountains makes for wonderful views, whether from terra firma or high above, aboard a cable car. Montjuïc and Park Güell offer multiple opportunities to look down upon this beautiful Mediterranean city, and there are lesser-known vantage points, too. Tibidabo, on the highest hill (512m) north of the city, has the best and most far-ranging views over Barcelona and out to the sea. Meanwhile, you'll find other rewarding views of the city in motion along La Rambla, from outdoor restaurants in Barceloneta and across plazas in the old city.

Best High-Altitude Views

Teleférico del Puerto Splendid views over the city and along the coast. (p181)

Bell Towers, La Sagrada Família A whole new perspective on Barcelona's most celebrated work in progress. (p111)

Park Güell Sweeping city views from the Turó del Calvari in the park's southwestern corner. (p114)

Mirador de Colom This monument surveys La Rambla, the old city and the waterfront. (pictured above; p27)

Castell de Montjuïc Fine views over the Montjuïc treetops to the city beyond. (p128)

Best for Iconic Barcelona

Park bench, La Rambla Watch the endlessly fascinating procession of the world's peoples. (p24)

La Pedrera rooftop Gaudí's fantastical chimney pots with stately Passeig de Gràcia behind. (p91)

Mercat de la Boqueria The best views of the market are from the Museu de l'Eròtica. (p46)

Best Eating & Drinking Views

La Caseta del Migdia An open-air charmer, hidden in the thickets of Montjuïc. (p133)

La Vinya del Senyor At night, wine in hand, beneath the floodlit Basílica de Santa Maria del Mar. (p73)

Barraca Dine on first-rate seafood while contemplating the deep-blue Mediterranean. (p86)

Best
Museums

With such a rich heritage of art and architecture, few cities rival Barcelona's array of world-class museums. As always in Spain, the line between a museum and an art gallery is deliciously blurred; in this section we've concentrated on traditional museums that take you for a ride through the history of Catalonia and beyond, with detours into the world of art.

History Museums

You could easily spend weeks working your way through Barcelona's museums. At journey's end, if you've visited them all, you'll have been on an extraordinarily diverse adventure through the history of Barcelona and the wider Catalan region. The story of the layers of civilisation that have accumulated here, one atop the other, including the Jews and Romans, is a series of intriguing tales that add depth and context to your experience of the city. This being a port city par excellence, the story also leads further afield, with discourses on Barcelona's seafaring past that take in everything from Spain's former colonies to ethnological exhibits from cultures all across the world. From football to ceramics to civil war air-raid shelters, there's nowhere, it seems, that Barcelona's museums can't take you.

The History of Art

The arts loom large over so many aspects of Barcelona life, and the city's museums take up the story with aplomb. The breadth of subject matter is extraordinary, with modern architecture and Antoni Gaudí recurring themes. But where Barcelona's museums excel is in their preservation of Catalonia's unimaginably rich history of Romanesque art and architecture.

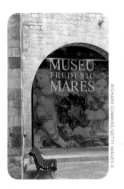

RICHARD CUMMINS/GETTY IMAGES ©

Best Journeys Through History

Museu d'Història de Barcelona Rich Roman ruins and Gothic architecture. (p34)

Museu d'Història de Catalunya A wonderfully composed ode to Catalan history. (p82)

Museu Marítim Barcelona as Mediterranean port city in the Gothic former shipyards. (p82)

Camp Nou Experience Learn about the history of the club, including dark episodes that involve assassination and kidnapping. (p136)

Museu Etnològic Discover Catalan traditions and rituals. (p130)

CosmoCaixa

MUHBA Refugi 307 Revisit wartime Barcelona in this evocative network of air-raid shelters. (p130)

Museu-Monestir de Pedralbes Window on monastic life and marvellous Gothic cloister. (p139)

Museu de l'Eròtica Observe what naughtiness people have been getting up to since ancient times. (p26)

Best Art History Museums

Museu Nacional d'Art de Catalunya Breathtaking Romanesque art and a peerless portfolio of Catalan artists. (p118)

Museu Frederic Marès Outstanding repository of Spanish sculpture, with Romanesque art the star. (pictured above left; p34)

Museu Gaudí Step inside Gaudí's mind and workshop with drawings and scale models. (p111)

Casa-Museu Gaudí Gaudí's one-time home in Park Güell. (p115)

Museu Olímpic i de l'Esport Fascinating survey of Olympian history. (p130)

◆ Worth a Trip

Kids (and many grown-ups) can't resist the interactive displays and experiments in **CosmoCaixa** (Museu de la Ciència; ☏93 212 60 50; www.fundacio. lacaixa.es; Carrer de Isaac Newton 26; adult/child €4/free; ⏰10am-8pm Tue-Sun; ☒60, ☒FGC Avinguda Tibidabo), a bright, playful science museum housed in a Modernista building at the foot of the Tibidabo hill. Think fossils, physics and an Amazonian rainforest.

Best
For Kids

From street performers who strut their stuff the length of La Rambla to art and architecture that looks like it emerged from a child's imagination, the sheer theatre of Barcelona's streets is a source of endless fascination for kids. Throw in an abundance of child-centric attractions (including beaches, pools and parks) and this is one city that seems made for a family holiday.

SEMSATCH/SHUTTERSTOCK ©

Child-Friendly Culture

One of the great things about Barcelona is the inclusion of children in many apparently adult activities. Going out to eat or sipping a beer on a late summer evening at a *terraza* needn't mean leaving children with minders. Locals take their kids out all the time and it's not unusual to see all ages, from toddlers to grandparents, enjoying the city until well into the night. A good starting point for what Barcelona has to offer for children can be found at www.kidsinbarcelona.com; its child-friendly listings are updated regularly.

Practical Matters

Most of the mid- and upper-range hotels in Barcelona can organise a babysitting service. Many hotels use **5 Serveis** (☎93 412 56 76; www.5serveis.com; Carrer de Pelai 50; Ⓜ Catalunya), which you can also contact directly. It has multilingual babysitters (*canguros*). Expect to pay at least €10 an hour plus a taxi fare home for the babysitter. If you're willing to let your kid share your bed, you won't incur a supplement in hotels. Extra beds usually (though not always) incur a €20 to €30 charge.

☑ Top Tips

▶ Adjust your children to Barcelona time (ie late nights), otherwise they'll miss half of what's worth seeing.

▶ Ask the local tourist office for the nearest children's playgrounds.

Best Attractions

L'Aquàrium One of Spain's best aquariums, with a shark tunnel and 11,000 fish. (p82)

Beaches Plenty of sand and gentle waters within walking distance.

Poble Espanyol A village in miniature that's guaranteed to capture the kids' attention. (p128)

Enjoying the views of Barcelona

Teleférico del Puerto
Exhilarating cable car that feels like a fairground ride. (p181)

Parc de la Ciutadella
Central Barcelona's largest park with ample space to play. (p68)

L'Anella Olímpica & Estadi Olímpic Swim the same pool as Olympic greats. (p129)

Camp Nou The football mad kid will never forget a visit here. (p136)

Best Museums

Museu de Cera Wax museum, complete with fairy-tale forest and time travel. (p27)

Museu Marítim Model ships, rafts and tall tales of the sea. (p82)

Castell de Montjuïc
Patrol the city ramparts. (p128)

Museu Olímpic i de l'Esport Sporty kids will love it. (p130)

Best for Fertile Imaginations

Park Güell Animals in glittering colours and Hansel and Gretel–like gatehouses. (p114)

Casa Batlló Architecture made for kids. (pictured above left; p92)

La Sagrada Família
Castle-like structure that seems to spring from a medieval legend. (p108)

Fundació Joan Miró
Children can relate to the childlike shapes and strong colours. (p122)

Worth a Trip

For the Ferris-wheel ride of your life, head for the **Parc d'Atraccions** (📞 93 211 79 42; www.tibidabo.cat; Plaça de Tibidabo 3-4; adult/child €30/11; 🕙 closed Jan & Feb; 🚌 T2A from Plaça de Catalunya), an old-fashioned funfair high on the Tibidabo hill. Getting here's half the fun, but always check the website for opening times before setting out.

Best
Tours

Tours certainly aren't necessary to enjoy Barcelona, but a handful of tours can enhance your visit, either by providing you with an introduction to the city or by zeroing in on an important aspect of Barcelona life that you simply couldn't access or understand on your own. Self-guided tours are another way to delve more deeply into a particular area of interest, such as the Ruta del Modernisme.

LITTLEADW/SHUTTERSTOCK ©

Barcelona Walking Tours

(☎93 285 38 34; www.barcelonaturisme.com; Plaça de Catalunya 17; Ⓜ Catalunya) The tourist office runs 17 themed walking tours that focus on the Barri Gòtic, Picasso's Barcelona, Modernisme and the city's food culture.

Bike Tours Barcelona

(☎93 268 21 05; www.biketoursbarcelona.com; Carrer de l'Esparteria 3; tour €22; ☺10am-7pm; Ⓜ Jaume I) One of numerous operators offering three-hour tours of the Barri Gòtic, waterfront, La Sagrada Família and other Gaudí landmarks. Turn up outside the tourist office on Plaça de Sant Jaume; check the website for departure times.

Las Golondrinas

(☎93 442 31 06; www.lasgolondrinas.com; Moll de les Drassanes; 40min tour adult/child €7.40/2.80; Ⓜ Drassanes) A seaborne perspective of the city with a 1½-hour jaunt around the harbour and along the beaches to the northeast tip of town. Shorter trips available.

GoCar

(☎93 269 17 92; www.gocartours.com; Passeig de Pujades 7; tours, min of 2, per person 1/2½/8hr €19/39/59; ☺10am-4pm Nov-Mar, 10am-6pm Apr-Oct; Ⓜ Arc de Triomf) GPS-guided, two-seat, three-wheeled moped cars with commentary as you zip around town. High on the novelty scale.

My Favourite Things

(☎637 265405; www.myft.net; tours from €26) Offers tours for no more than 10 participants based on numerous themes: anything from design to food. Other activities include flamenco and salsa classes and bicycle rides in and out of Barcelona.

Bus Turístic

(☎93 298 70 00; www.barcelonabusturistic.cat/en; day ticket adult/child €28/16; ☺9am-8pm) This hop-on, hop-off service covers virtually all of the city's main sights. Audioguides (in 10 languages) provide running commentary on the 44 stops on the three different circuits. Each of the two main circuits takes around two hours.

Ruta del Modernisme

For a self-guided tour that leads past 115 Modernista buildings, pick up this book and map (€12) at the main tourist office on Plaça de Catalunya. (see boxed text, p98)

Best
For Free

There are so many museums in Barcelona that seeing even a small portion of them can seem like a major financial investment. But a series of combination tickets help keep costs down, and some of Barcelona's top attractions charge no admission, while others have free periods.

Free Days

Most government-run museums open their doors without charge on the first Sunday of every month. On other Sundays, most refrain from charging from 3pm to 8pm. And of course you pay no admission fee for attractions like markets, gardens and beaches.

Take a Walk

They're not technically free, but numerous companies offer pay-what-you-wish walking tours. These typically take in the Barri Gòtic or the Modernista sites of L'Eixample. A few recommended outfitters include Runner Bean Tours, Feel Free Tours and Travel Bound.

Check websites for meeting places and departure times.

Best Always Free

L'Anella Olímpica & Estadi Olímpic Relive unforgettable Olympic moments. (p129)

Temple Romà d'August Towering vestiges of Roman glory in the centre of old Barcelona. (p34)

Antic Hospital de la Santa Creu Wander into the grand Gothic reading room. (p51)

Best Free Days for Top Museums

Museu Nacional d'Art de Catalunya Free 3pm to 8pm on Saturdays and all day on the first Sunday of the month. (p118)

Museu Picasso Free 3pm to 7pm every Sunday and all day on the first Sunday of the month. (p58)

Museu d'Història de Barcelona Free 3pm to 8pm every Sunday and all day on the first Sunday of the month. (p34)

Museu d'Història de Catalunya Free on the last Tuesday of the month between October and June. (p82)

CaixaForum Free on the first Sunday of the month. (pictured above; p128)

La Catedral Free every day from 8am to 12.45pm and 5.15pm to 8pm. (p28)

Best
Bars

Barcelona is a nightlife-lovers' town, with an enticing spread of candlelit wine bars, old-school taverns and stylish lounges where the festivities continue late into the night. The atmosphere varies tremendously – shadowy mural-covered chambers in the medieval quarter, antique-filled converted storefronts and buzzing Modernista spaces are all part of the scene.

PHOTOSMATIC/SHUTTERSTOCK ©

Bar Neighbourhoods

There are bars on just about every street corner in Barcelona, and every neighbourhood has its local watering hole. But the densest concentrations of dedicated drinking dens are to be found in the Barri Gòtic, El Raval, La Ribera (particularly El Born) and L'Eixample.

Wine & Cava Bars

A growing number of wine bars scattered around the city provide a showcase for the great produce from Spain and beyond. Vine-minded spots serve a huge selection of wines by the glass, with a particular focus on stellar new vintages. A big part of the experience is having a few bites while you drink. Expect sharing plates, platters of cheese and charcuterie, and plenty of tapas.

Beach Bars

During summer small wooden beach bars, affectionately known as *chiringuitos*, open up along the strand, from Barceloneta all the way up to Platja de la Nova Mar Bella. Here you can dig your heels in the sand, grab a snack and nurse a sangria (pictured above), or some fresh-squeezed juice while watching the city at play against the backdrop of the Mediterranean.

Best Bars with History

Casa Almirall Barcelona's oldest continuously functioning bar with wonderful period detail. (p54)

Bar Marsella They've seen it all at this gritty 19th-century El Raval bar. (p49)

La Confitería Fin-de-siècle spot in El Raval that pours a fine house vermouth. (p53)

Les Gens Que J'Aime Romantic relic of 1960s L'Eixample with candlelight and red-velvet sofas. (p105)

A local bar in El Born

Best Local Bars

Vaso de Oro Barceloneta as it used to be. (p79)

Rubí Great drink specials hidden away on a narrow lane in El Born. (p73)

Best Cocktail Bars

Dry Martini Suited waiters and perfect dry martinis in L'Eixample. (p105)

Juanra Falces White jacketed waiters serve up artful elixirs. (p74)

Best for Style

Ocaña Sitting pretty on Plaça Reial with a beautifully designed interior. (p40)

Sor Rita Join festive crowds in a whimsical Almódovar-esque world. (p40)

Best Wine Bars

Monvínic With over 3000 wines to choose from, you won't lack for options. (p95)

La Vinya del Senyor More than 350 wines and a perfect setting. (p73)

Best Cava Bars

El Xampanyet Nowhere does the tapas-*cava* combination better than this 1930s-era El Born bar. (p65)

Can Paixano Ageless Barceloneta *cava* den of sheer raucous pleasure. (p78)

Best Music Bar

Bar Pastís Shoebox-sized bar with music from French cabaret to tango. (p54)

Best Bohemian Hang-Outs

Gran Bodega Saltó Psychedelic decor, live music and an eclectic crowd. (p125)

Absenta Absinthe-fuelled drinking den with whimsical scultpures. (p86)

Gipsy Lou Festive any-time spot on the Plaça de George Orwell. (p55)

Tinta Roja Atmospheric El Raval drinking den with live music and other events from time to time. (p125)

El Rouge Bordello-esque bar known for its surreal performances. (p125)

Best
Cafes

Barcelona is distinguished by its historic cafes, where bow-tied waiters and period interiors are de rigeur. Many have been discovered by tourists, but you're still likely to find two men playing chess as they have done for decades, or a wizened old-timer, glass of cognac in hand, simply watching the world go by.

DIEGO LEZAMA/GETTY IMAGES ©

The Best of the Old

The Modernistas and others of their architectural ilk didn't content themselves with exotic facades: just as often, the city's architects put as much effort into adorning the interiors of the city's salons. Such is the backdrop for many a Barcelona cafe. But in this city that seems hell-bent on redefining the future, it's the atmosphere in these cafes – the clientele and the decor – that serves to remind us that this is also a profoundly traditional city. Here, an older way of doing things prevails – a mid-morning coffee or something stronger, long hours spent solving the problems of the world with friends. And therein lies the raison d'être of Barcelona's cafes: these are meeting places and hubs of social life, and have been for centuries.

In with the New

This being Barcelona, slick new cafes have also found a place in the affections of *barcelonins*. These are the sort of places where you sit beneath contemporary artworks as you update your Facebook profile to a soundtrack of lounge and other chill-out music, where the waiters are young and friendly, and where you're just as likely to encounter cocktails as coffee.

☑ Top Tips

▶ For sweet teeth, head for a *granja* (milk bar), where thick hot chocolate is the go. Cafe-lined Carrer de Petritxol in the Barri Gòtic is famed for its chocolate options.

▶ A *café con leche* is a white coffee, *café solo* is an espresso, and a *cortado* is an espresso with a small amount of milk.

Chocolate crêpes

Best Historic Cafes

Cafè de l'Òpera A grand old art-deco dame of La Rambla, going strong since 1929. (p25)

Mauri Another from the class of 1929, with an ornate fresco and classy L'Eixample clientele. (p95)

Salterio Candles and old stone walls make for a mesmerising atmosphere at this spot in the former Jewish quarter. (p40)

Caelum Temptations of all sorts, best enjoyed in the medieval chamber in the basement. (p40)

Best Local Cafes

La Nena Hot chocolate, crêpes and desserts draw in a mix of Gràcia hipsters and young families. (p113)

Cosmo Archetypal modern art cafe – cool, chilled, and offering creative coffees and teas. (p95)

Bar Kasparo Great place to linger, with a peaceful setting overlooking a leafy plaza. (p48)

Federal Aussie-run cafe and eating spot with a pleasant roof terrace. (p125)

Best Chocolate

Granja M Viader Spain's most popular chocolate drink was invented in this 19th-century classic. (p49)

Granja La Pallaresa Leading candidate for Barcelona's best coffee or hot chocolate in the Barri Gòtic. (p31)

Foix de Sarrià A 19th-century pastry shop in Sarrià of chocolatey decadence and hot drinks. (p140)

Cacao Sampaka Chocolate lovers go weak at the knees at this L'Eixample icon. (p95)

Best
Clubs

Barcelona's reputation as a party town is well deserved, although many of the better places are found in La Zona Alta, the upmarket suburbs north of the centre. If you can't move that far, there are options closer to the centre. A surprising variety of spots lurk in the old-town labyrinth, ranging from plush former dance halls to grungy subterranean venues. Along the waterfront it's another story: at Port Olímpic sun-scorched crowds of visiting yachties mix it up with tourists and a few locals at noisy, back-to-back dance bars right on the waterfront.

CHRISTIAN BERTRAND/SHUTTERSTOCK ©

Best Clubs

La Terrrazza Outdoor summer-only Montjuïc venue filled with top DJs and Barcelona's beautiful people. (p133)

Moog Techno, electronica, retro pop and big-name DJs ensure a packed El Raval dance floor. (p55)

Marula Café Best choice for a young crowd in the Barri Gòtic. (p41)

Antilla BCN Barcelona's premier club for salsa and sexy Cuban tunes. (p105)

Ocaña The downstairs lounge hosts good DJs on weekends. (p40)

Best Live-Gig Clubs

Jamboree DJ-spun hip hop and funk on Plaça Reial. (p42)

Sala Apolo House, techno and the like with an eclectic crowd. (p125)

☑ **Top Tips**

▶ Clubs typically open from midnight to 6am Thursday to Saturday. Things are pretty dead before 2am.

▶ Cover charges range from nothing to upwards of €20. The admission price usually includes your first drink.

▶ Dress well to get past the bouncers. If you're in a big group, break into smaller groups.

▶ Browse the latest on Barcelona Rocks (www.barcelona rocks.com), Clubbing Spain (www.clubbing spain.com) and Guía del Ocio (www.guia delocio.com).

Best LGBT

With a busy gay and lesbian scene, this is one of the most gay-friendly cities in southern Europe. The bulk of the action happens in 'Gaixample', the five or six blocks of L'Eixample bounded by Gran Via de les Corts Catalanes, Carrer de Balmes, Carrer del Consell de Cent and Carrer de Casanova.

INGRID PRATS/SHUTTERSTOCK ©

Best Bars

La Chapelle (☑93 453 30 76; Carrer de Muntaner 67; ◔4pm-2am Sun-Thu, to 2.30am Fri & Sat; ⓂUniversitat) Relaxed meeting place with provocative religious decor that welcomes all.

Aire (Sala Diana; ☑93 487 83 42; www.grupoarena.com; Carrer de la Diputació 233; ◔11pm-2.30am Thu-Sat; ⓂPasseig de Gràcia) Popular spot for lesbians with a spacious dance floor.

Átame (☑93 421 41 33; Carrer del Consell de Cent 257; ◔9pm-2.30am; ⓂUniversitat) Chat over drinks early, stay late as things heat up.

Museum (Carrer de Sepúlveda 178; ◔11pm-3am Tue-Sat; ⓂUniversitat) Lots of kitschy fun to be had at this so-called 'video bar'.

Punto BCN (☑93 451 91 52; www.grupoarena.com; Carrer de Muntaner 63-65; ◔6pm-2.30am Sun-Thu, to 3am Fri & Sat; ⓂUniversitat) A two-level bar with a good mix of ages and creeds.

Bacon Bear (Carrer de Casanova 64; ◔6pm-2.30am Mon-Thu, 6pm-3am Fri & Sat; ⓂUrgell) Burly folk and their admirers.

Best Clubs

Arena Madre (☑93 487 83 42; www.grupoarena.com; Carrer de Balmes 32; ◔12.30-5am; ⓂPasseig de Gràcia) One of the top clubs in town for boys seeking boys.

Metro (☑93 323 52 27; www.metrodiscobcn.com; Carrer de Sepúlveda 185; from €6 before 2am, €20 after 2am; ◔12.15am-5.30am; ⓂUniversitat) Topnotch DJs preside over

☑ Top Tips

▶ The southern end of Platja de la Mar Bella, located north of Barceloneta, is a gay-male nudist strip from mid-afternoon.

▶ Most clubs open only from Thursday to Saturday nights.

▶ Find events at 60by80 (www.60by80.com) and Gay Barcelona (www.gaybarcelona.com).

two heaving dance floors and other amusements.

Pervert Club (Avinguda Francesc Ferrer i Guàrdia 13 ◔ ⓂEspanya) midnight-6am Sat Riotously good fun at this Saturday-night party held inside a club called The One in Poble Espanyol.

Best
Live Music & the Arts

BARBARA VAN ZANTEN/GETTY IMAGES ©

Barcelona is an important stop for most musicians on any European tour. You'll also find home-grown talents that meld flamenco and rumba with rap, ragga and electronica. But even the weekly diet of jazz, leavened with a little rock, flamenco and blues, keeps locals happy.

Best Live Jazz & Other Music

Harlem Jazz Club One of Barcelona's best-known jazz stages, with a handy Barri Gòtic location. (p42)

Jamboree A fine jazz venue on Plaça Reial that draws big talent. (p42)

Jazz Sí Club Eclectic line-up of live music, including flamenco, Cuban jazz, rock and blues. (p49)

Sala Apolo Alternative mix of offbeat rock acts, world music and DJs. (p125)

La Pedrera Summertime concerts on the rooftop of a Gaudí masterpiece. (p90)

Plaça Nova *Sardana* (Catalan folk dancing) in front of La Catedral at 6pm Saturdays and 11am Sundays. (p31)

Montjuïc Every Sunday from June through September, enjoy a day of electronic music at an outdoor space on Montjuïc (www.piknic electronik.es).

Best High Culture

Palau de la Música Catalana Modernista auditorium, staging everything from classical music to Spanish guitar. (p68)

Gran Teatre del Liceu World-class opera, an extravagant setting and fine acoustics. (p27)

Survival Guide

Survival Guide

Before You Go

When to Go

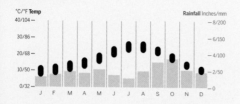

→ Summer (Jun–Aug)
Hot beach weather, but often overwhelmed with visitors in July and August; locals escape the city in August.

→ Autumn (Sep–Nov)
September is one of the best months to visit; chance of rain in October and November.

→ Winter (Dec–Feb)
Nights can be chilly and there's a chance of rain, but there are fewer visitors and sunny days are possible.

→ Spring (Mar–May) A lovely time to visit. Manageable visitor numbers, though rain is possible in April and May.

Book Your Stay

☑ **Top Tip** If you arrive without prebooked lodging, Plaça de Catalunya's tourist office can help.

→ Accommodation in Barcelona is at a premium year-round so always book as far in advance as possible.

→ Barcelona's price-to-quality ratio is generally high, but prices can double on weekends and during important festivals and trade fairs.

→ Staying in the Barri Gòtic, El Raval or La Ribera puts you in the heart of the action, but nights can be noisy and long from Thursday through the weekend.

→ L'Eixample can be quieter (assuming you're not on a busy boulevard), while Barceloneta is perfect if you're here for the beach.

Useful Websites

Lonely Planet (www.lonelyplanet.com) Neighbourhood profiles, plus extensive listings of hotels, hostels, guesthouses and apartments.

Oh Barcelona (www.oh-barcelona.com) Hotel and apartment listings, plus tips on deciding where to stay.

Barcelona Bed and Breakfasts (www.barcelonabedandbreakfasts.com) Listings of low-key, oft-overlooked lodging options.

Best Budget

Casa Gràcia (www.casagraciabcn.com) Stylish hostel with colourful rooms, communal dinners, film screenings and other events.

Amistat Beach Hostel (www.amistatbeachhostel.com) Small, warm and welcoming hostel, near the beach and restaurants of Poblenou.

Tailor's Hostel (www.tailors-hostel.com) A hip Sant Antoni option with a vintage vibe.

Chic & Basic Ramblas (www.chicandbasic.com)

Boasts serious design cred – particularly the lobby with its vintage decor.

Pars Teatro Hostel (www.teatrohostel.com) Theatrically decorated space on the edge of Poble Sec.

Pensió 2000 (www.pensio2000.com) This family-run place has reasonably spacious doubles with mosaic-tiled floors and en suite bathrooms.

Best Midrange

Hotel Brummell (www.hotelbrummell.com) A stylish Poble Sec stay with soul.

Five Rooms (www.thefiverooms.com) Small and charming option in L'Eixample.

Cami Bed & Gallery (www.camibedandgallery.com) Seven unique rooms in an art-filled Modernista building.

Hotel Market (www.andilanahotels.com) Beautifully designed rooms in the very hot 'hood of Sant Antoni.

H10 Port Vell (www.h10hotels.com) A plush stay in a great location

with Barceloneta and El Born near your doorstep.

Hotel Constanza (www.hotelconstanza.com) A boutique L'Eixample hotel with thoughtful details and an appealing terrace.

Best Top End

Cotton House (www.hotelcottonhouse.com) A beautifully designed L'Eixample hotel – you won't want to leave.

Serras Hotel (www.hoteltheserrasbarcelona.com) Luxurious lodging in an ideal Barri Gòtic location.

Hotel Neri (www.hotelneri.com) Beautiful, historic hotel on a tranquil spot in the Barri Gòtic.

Hotel Casa Fuster (www.hotelcasafuster.com) A photogenic Gràcia mansion with striking interiors.

DO (www.hoteldoreial.com) Magnificent boutique option overlooking Plaça Reial in the Barri Gòtic.

Grand Hotel Central (www.grandhotelcentral.com) Lovely spacious rooms and a rooftop infinity pool.

Arriving in Barcelona

☑ **Top Tip** For the best way to get to your accommodation, see p17.

Aeroport del Prat

Barcelona's **El Prat Airport** (☎902 404704; www.aena.es) lies 17km southwest of Plaça de Catalunya at El Prat de Llobregat. The airport has two main terminal buildings: the new T1 terminal and the older T2, itself divided into three terminal areas (A, B and C). The main **tourist office** (⏰8.30am-8.30pm) is on the ground floor of Terminal 2B. Other offices on the ground floor of Terminal 2A and in Terminal 1 operate the same hours.

➡ The **A1 Aerobús** (☎902 100104; www.aerobusbcn.com; one way/return €5.90/10.20; ⏰6am-1am) runs from Terminal 1 to Plaça de Catalunya (30 to 40 minutes depending on traffic) via Plaça d'Espanya, Gran Via de les Corts Catalanes and Plaça de la Universitat every five to 10 minutes from 6.10am to 1.05am.

➡ The **R2 Nord** train (one-way €4.50; from 5.42am to 11.38pm) leaves every half-hour from the airport via several stops to Barcelona's main train station, Estació de Sants (20 minutes) and Passeig de Gràcia (25 to 30 minutes) in central Barcelona. The airport railway station is about a five-minute walk from Terminal 2.

➡ A taxi to the centre (around 30 minutes, depending on traffic) costs €25 to €30.

Aeroport de Girona–Costa Brava

Girona–Costa Brava Airport (www.girona-airport.net) is 12km south of Girona and 92km northeast of Barcelona. You'll find a tourist office, ATMs and lost-luggage desks on the ground floor.

➡ **Sagalés** (☎902 130014; www.sagales.com) runs the Barcelona Bus (www.barcelonabus.com) service between Girona airport and Estació del Nord bus station in Barcelona (one-way/return €16/25, 75 minutes).

Aeroport de Reus

Reus Airport (☎902 404704; www.aena.es) is 13km west of Tarragona and 108km southwest of Barcelona. The tourist office and lost-luggage desks are in the main terminal building.

➡ **Hispano-Igualadina** (☎93 339 73 29; www.igualadina.com; Carrer de Viriat; Ⓜ Estació Sants) bus services run between Reus airport and Estació d'Autobusos de Sants to meet flights (90 minutes, one-way €16, 1½ hours).

Getting Around

Bicycle

☑ **Best for...** Scenic seaside rides.

➡ Barcelona has over 180km of bike lanes.

➡ A waterfront path runs northeast from Barceloneta to Port Olímpic and onwards to Riu Besòs.

➡ There are numerous places to hire bikes, particularly in the Barri Gòtic and La Ribera. Note that the red 'Bicing' hire bikes are available for Barcelona residents only.

➡ You can transport your bicycle on the metro on weekdays (except between 7am and 9.30am, and 5pm and 8.30pm). On weekends, holidays, and during July and August, there are no restrictions.

Bus

☑ **Best for...** Night trips.

→ **Transports Metro-politans de Barcelona** (TMB; ☎93 298 70 00; www.tmb.net) buses run from 5am or 6am to as late as 11pm, depending on the line. Many routes pass through Plaça de Catalunya and/or Plaça de la Universitat.

→ After 11pm a reduced network of yellow *nitbusos* (night buses) runs until 3am or 5am. All *nitbus* routes pass through Plaça de Catalunya and most run every 30 to 45 minutes. Single tickets cost €2.15 and can be purchased on the bus.

FGC

☑ **Best for...** Trips from Plaça de Catalunya to scattered attractions such as Tibidabo, Sarrià and Pedralbes.

→ The FGC (www.fgc.net) suburban rail network goes numerous places that the metro doesn't. It operates on a similar schedule and a one-way ticket costs €2.15.

Cable Cars

☑ **Best for...** Getting to and around Montjuïc.

→ Cable cars connect Barceloneta and Poble Sec with Montjuïc.

→ The **Teleférico del Puerto** (Map p80; www.telefericodebarcelona.com; Passeig Escullera; one way/return €11/16.50; ☺11am-7pm Mar-Oct, to 5.30pm Nov-Feb; ☐17, 39, 64, ⓜBarceloneta) service runs from the Torre de Sant Sebastià (in Barceloneta) to Miramar (on Montjuïc).

→ The funicular railway runs from the Paral·lel metro stop to the Estació Parc Montjuïc and is part of the metro ticketing system.

→ The **Telefèric de Montjuïc** (www.teleferic demontjuic.cat; Av de Miramar 30; adult/child one way €8/6.20; ☺10am-9pm Jun-Sep, to 7pm Oct-May; ☐55, 150) runs from the Estació Parc Montjuïc to the Castell de Montjuïc at the summit of Montjuïc.

Metro

☑ **Best for...** Getting just about anywhere in the city, with an extensive network of lines and stations throughout the city. Exceptions include travel to Montjuïc and Sarrià.

→ **Transports Metro-politans de Barcelona** (TMB; ☎93 298 70 00; www.tmb.net) runs the metro system with eight colour-coded lines.

→ Single tickets, good for one journey no matter how many changes you have to make, cost €2.15 and can be bought at metro stations.

→ Save money by buying a Targeta T-10 (€10.30) – allowing 10 rides (each valid for 1¼ hours) on the metro, buses and FGC trains.

→ The metro operates from 5am to midnight Sunday to Thursday, from 5am to 2am on Friday, and all night Saturday.

Taxi

☑ **Top Tip Best for...** Quick trips across town (outside peak hour) and for late-night travel.

→ Taxis are reasonably priced and charges are posted on passenger-side windows inside.

→ You can call a taxi or flag one down in the street. Reliable operators include **Fonotaxi** (☎93 300 11 00) and **Radio Taxi 033** (☎93 303 30 33; http://radiotaxi033.com).

Essential Information

Business Hours

☑ Smaller shops in Barcelona close for an extended siesta, typically between 2pm and 4.30pm or 5pm.

Banks 8.30am-2pm Mon-Fri; some also 4-7pm Thu and 9am-1pm Sat

Central Post Offices 8.30am-9.30pm Mon-Fri, 8.30am-2pm Sat

Restaurants lunch 1-4pm, dinner 8pm-midnight

Shops 10am-2pm and 4.30-7.30pm or 5-8pm

Discount Cards

☑ **Top Tip** A great deal for culture lovers, Articket BCN (p52) gives admission to six museums for €30.

The following cards (except student cards) are available at tourist offices:

ArqueoTicket (€13 per person) Entry to four museums (Museu d'Història de Barcelona, Museu d'Arqueologia de Catalunya, Museu Egipci and Born Centre de Cultura i Memòria).

Barcelona Card (www.barcelonacard.com; 2/3/5 days €35/45/60) Free transport (and 20% off the Aerobús) and discounted admission (up to 30% off) or free entry to many sights. Cheaper if you book online, and kids' versions are available.

Ruta del Modernisme (www.rutadelmodernisme.com; €12) Discounts at Barcelona's main Modernista sights.

Student Cards Discounts of up to 50% at many sights.

Electricity

220V/230V/50Hz

Emergency

Ambulance ☎061

EU Standard Emergency Number ☎112

Fire ☎080 or ☎085

Police (Mossos d'Esquadra) ☎088

Money

The Spanish currency is the euro (€), divided into 100 cents.

ATMs Widely available; there is usually a charge on ATM cash withdrawals abroad.

Cash Banks and building societies offer the best rates; take your passport for ID.

Credit & Debit Cards Accepted in most hotels, restaurants and shops. May need to show passport or an alternative photo ID.

Public Holidays

Many shops will be closed and many attractions operate on reduced hours on the following dates:

New Year's Day 1 January

Epiphany 6 January

Good Friday Late March/April

Easter Monday Late March/April

Labour Day 1 May

Dilluns de Pasqua Grande (day after Pentecost Sunday) May/June

Feast of St John the Baptist 24 June

Feast of the Assumption 15 August

Catalonia's National Day 11 September

Festes de la Mercè 24 September

Spain's National Day 12 October

All Saints' Day 1 November

Constitution Day 6 December

Feast of the Immaculate Conception 8 December

Christmas Day 25 December

St Stephen's Day (Boxing Day) 26 December

Safe Travel

Petty crime and theft, with tourists the prey of choice, is a problem in Barcelona, although most visitors encounter few problems. Take particular care on airport trains, the metro (especially around stops popular with tourists) and La Rambla.

Telephone

Mobile Phones

➡ Local SIM cards are widely available and can be used in European and Australian mobile phones.

➡ US travellers will need to set their phones to roaming, or buy a local mobile and SIM card.

Phone Codes

Country code ☏ 34

International access code ☏ 00

Toilets

There are few public toilets in Barcelona, and cafes and bars are your best bet when in need. Make sure your chosen bar actually has a toilet before committing yourself.

Tourist Information

The Turisme de Barcelona (www.barcelonaturisme. com) has offices around the city:

Plaça de Catalunya (Map p50; ☏ 93 285 38 34; Plaça de Catalunya 17; ◷ 9.30am-9.30pm; Ⓜ Catalunya) Main office.

Barri Gòtic (Map p32; ☏ 93 285 38 32; Carrer de la Ciutat 2; ◷ 8.30am-8.30pm Mon-Fri, 9am-7pm Sat, 9am-2pm Sun & holidays; Ⓜ Jaume I)

Dos & Don'ts

Eating and drinking Waiters won't expect you to thank them every time they bring you something, but they will expect you to keep your cutlery between courses in more casual restaurants and bars.

Escalators Always stand on the right to let people pass, especially when using the metro.

Greetings Catalans, like other Spaniards, usually greet friends and strangers alike with a kiss on both cheeks, although two males rarely do this. Foreigners may be excused.

Visiting churches It is considered disrespectful to visit churches as a tourist during Mass and other worship services. Taking photos at such times is a definite no-no.

Money-Saving Tips

➡ Look out for free entry at sights.

➡ Order the *menú del día* (daily set menu) for lunch in restaurants.

➡ Buy discount cards.

➡ Buy 10-trip travel cards to get around the city.

Estació Sants (Estació Sants; ⏱8am-8pm; 🚆Estació Sants)

Aeroport del Prat (⏱8.30am-8.30pm)

Travellers with Disabilities

➡ Some hotels and many public institutions have wheelchair access.

➡ All buses and a growing number of metro stations are wheelchair accessible.

➡ Metro lines 2, 9, 10 and 11 are completely adapted, as are the majority of stops on line 1.

➡ Ticket vending machines in metro stations are adapted for the disabled and have Braille options for the blind.

Accessible Barcelona (www.accessible barcelona.com) has useful info on accessing key sites, though it isn't updated regularly.

Several taxi companies have adapted vehicles including **Taxi Amic** (☎93 420 80 88; www.taxi-amic-adaptat.com) and **Gestverd** (☎93 303 09 09; www. gestverd.com).

Visas

EU & Schengen Countries No visa required.

Australia, Canada, Israel, Japan, New Zealand and the USA No visa required for tourist visits of up to 90 days.

Other Countries Check with a Spanish embassy or consulate.

Language

Both Catalan (*català*) and Spanish (more precisely known as *castellano*, or Castilian) have official language status in Catalonia. In Barcelona you'll hear as much Spanish as Catalan and you'll find that most locals will happily speak Spanish to you, especially once they realise you're a foreigner. In this chapter, we've provided you with some Spanish to get you started, as well as some Catalan basics at the end.

Just read our pronunciation guides as if they were English and you'll be understood. Note that (m/f) indicates masculine and feminine forms.

To enhance your trip with a phrase-book, visit **lonelyplanet.com**. Lonely Planet iPhone phrasebooks are available through the Apple App store.

Basics

Hello.
Hola.   o·la

Goodbye.
Adiós.   a·dyos

How are you?
¿Qué tal?   ke tal

Fine, thanks.
Bien, gracias.   byen gra·thyas

Please.
Por favor.   por fa·vor

Thank you.
Gracias.   gra·thyas

Excuse me.
Perdón.   per·don

Sorry.
Lo siento.   lo syen·to

Yes./No.
Sí./No.   see/no

Do you speak (English)?
¿Habla (inglés)?   a·bla (een·gles)

I (don't) understand.
Yo (no) entiendo.   yo (no) en·tyen·do

Eating & Drinking

I'm a vegetarian. (m/f)
Soy   soy
vegetariano/a.   ve·khe·ta·rya·no/a

Cheers!
¡Salud!   sa·loo

That was delicious!
¡Estaba   es·ta·ba
buenísimo!   bwe·nee·see·mo

Please bring the bill.
Por favor nos   por fa·vor nos
trae la cuenta.   tra·e la kwen·ta

I'd like ...
Quisiera ...   kee·sye·ra ...

a coffee	un café	oon ka·fe
a table for two	una mesa para dos	oo·na me·sa pa·ra dos
a wine	un vino	oon vee·no
two beers	dos cervezas	dos ther·ve·thas

Shopping

I'd like to buy ...
Quisiera   kee·sye·ra
comprar ...   kom·prar ...

May I look at it?
¿Puedo verlo?   pwe·do ver·lo

How much is it?
¿Cuánto cuesta?   kwan·to kwes·ta

That's too/very expensive.
Es muy caro.   es mooy ka·ro

Can you lower the price?
¿Podría bajar   po·dree·a ba·khar
un poco   oon po·ko
el precio?   el pre·thyo

Emergencies

Help!
¡Socorro! — so·ko·ro

Call a doctor!
¡Llame a — lya·me a oon
un médico! — me·dee·ko

Call the police!
¡Llame a — lya·me a
la policía! — la po·lee·*thee*·a

I'm lost. (m/f)
Estoy perdido/a. — es·toy per·dee·do/a

I'm ill. (m/f)
Estoy enfermo/a. — es·toy en·*fer*·mo/a

Where are the toilets?
¿Dónde están — don·de es·tan
los baños? — los ba·nyos

Time & Numbers

What time is it?
¿Qué hora es? — ke o·ra es

It's (10) o'clock.
Son (las diez). — son (las dyeth)

morning	*mañana*	ma·*nya*·na
afternoon	*tarde*	tar·de
evening	*noche*	no·che
yesterday	*ayer*	a·yer
today	*hoy*	oy
tomorrow	*mañana*	ma·*nya*·na

1	*uno*	oo·no
2	*dos*	dos
3	*tres*	tres
4	*cuatro*	kwa·tro
5	*cinco*	*theen*·ko
6	*seis*	seys
7	*siete*	*sye*·te
8	*ocho*	o·cho
9	*nueve*	*nwe*·ve
10	*diez*	dyeth

Transport & Directions

Where's ...?
¿Dónde está ...? — don·de es·ta ...

What's the address?
¿Cuál es la — kwal es la
dirección? — dee·rek·*thyon*

Can you show me (on the map)?
¿Me lo puede — me lo *pwe*·de
indicar — een·dee·*kar*
(en el mapa)? — (en el *ma*·pa)

I want to go to ...
Quisiera ir a ... — kee·*sye*·ra eer a ...

What time does it arrive/leave?
¿A qué hora — a ke o·ra
llega/sale? — *lye*·ga/sa·le

I want to get off here.
Quiero bajarme — *kye*·ro ba·*khar*·me
aquí. — a·*kee*

Catalan – Basics

Good morning.
Bon dia. — bon dee·a

Good afternoon.
Bona tarda. — bo·na tar·da

Good evening.
Bon vespre. — bon bes·pra

Goodbye.
Adéu. — a·*the*·oo

Please.
Sisplau. — sees·*pla*·oo

Thank you.
Gràcies. — gra·see·a

You're welcome.
De res. — de res

Excuse me.
Perdoni. — par·*tho*·nee

I'm sorry.
Ho sento. — oo sen·to

How are you?
Com estàs? — kom as·tas

Very well.
(Molt) Bé. — (mol) be

Behind the Scenes

Send Us Your Feedback

We love to hear from travellers – your comments help make our books better. We read every word, and we guarantee that your feedback goes straight to the authors. Visit **lonelyplanet.com/contact** to submit your updates and suggestions.

Note: We may edit, reproduce and incorporate your comments in Lonely Planet products such as guidebooks, websites and digital products, so let us know if you don't want your comments reproduced or your name acknowledged. For a copy of our privacy policy visit lonelyplanet.com/privacy.

Our Readers

Many thanks to the travellers who used the last edition and wrote to us with helpful hints, useful advice and interesting anecdotes: Iain Whitmey

Regis' Thanks

I'm grateful to the many friends and acquaintances who provided guidance and tips along the way. Biggest thanks go to co-author Sal Davies for all her assistance, including the temporary crash pad, and to kind hosts Xabi and Lucia in El Born. Thanks also to Cristiano Nogueira for making the detour from France. Finally, big hugs to my family for all their support.

Sally's Thanks

Thanks chiefly go to my Barcelona support team, especially Mary-Ann Gallagher and Matthew Wrigley, but also Sarah Davison, Aurélie Herrou, Jane Darroch and John O'Donovan. Thanks to Regis St Louis for fielding questions and sharing intel, and hat tip to foodies Buster Turner, Paul Richardson and Llibert Figueras for some excellent lunches. Extra special thanks to Tess, for putting up with it all.

Acknowledgements

Cover photograph: Casa Batlló, Jordan Banks/4Corners©.
Contents photograph: The Roof Terrace, La Pedrera, Christopher Groenhout/Lone/Getty©.

This Book

This 5th edition of Lonely Planet's *Pocket Barcelona* guidebook was researched and written by Regis St Louis and Sally Davies. The previous edition was also written by Regis St Louis. This guidebook was produced by the following:
Destination Editors Lorna Parkes, Clifton Wilkinson
Product Editors Kate Mathews, Jenna Myers
Senior Cartographer Anthony Phelan
Cartographer James Leversha
Book Designer Wendy Wright
Assisting Editor Gabrielle Stefanos
Cover Researcher Naomi Parker
Thanks to Grace Dobell, Liz Heynes, Susan Paterson, Kirsten Rawlings, Luna Soo, Angela Tinson, Tony Wheeler

Index

See also separate subindexes for:

⊗ **Eating p190**

🍴 **Drinking p191**

✪ **Entertainment p191**

🔒 **Shopping p191**

Our Writers

Regis St Louis

Regis fell in love with Barcelona a decade ago, after arriving in the city and being awestruck by its wild architecture, culinary creativity and warm-hearted people. Since then he has returned frequently, learning Spanish and a smattering of Catalan, and delving into the endless layers of Barcelona's deep cultural heritage. Favourite memories from his most recent trip include fêting the arrival of three bearded kings during Dia de Reis, catching a surreal circus arts show in a seaside suburb, and exploring far-flung corners of Montjuïc at sunrise. Regis is the author of the previous edition of *Pocket Barcelona*, and he has contributed to *Spain*, *Portugal* and dozens of other Lonely Planet titles.

Sally Davies

Sally landed in Seville in 1992 with a handful of pesetas and five words of Spanish, and, despite a complete inability to communicate, promptly snared a lucrative gig handing out leaflets at Expo '92. In 2001 she settled in Barcelona, where she is still incredulous that her daily grind involves researching fine restaurants, wandering about museums and finding ways to convey the beauty of this spectacular city.

Published by Lonely Planet Global Limited
CRN 554153
5th edition – Nov 2016
ISBN 978 1 78657 210 3
© Lonely Planet 2016   Photographs © as indicated 2016
10 9 8 7 6 5 4
Printed in Malaysia